# Interior Decoration

# *Interior Decoration*

POEMS BY

54 WOMEN

FROM 10 LANGUAGES

*Editors*

AMMU JOSEPH • VASANTH KANNABIRAN

• RITU MENON • VOLGA

WW (India)

Women Unlimited

*Interior Decoration: Poems by 54 Women from 10 Languages*
was first published in India in 2010 by

**Women Unlimited**
**(an associate of Kali for Women)**
**K-36, Hauz Khas Enclave, Ground Floor**
**New Delhi 110 016**

**in collaboration with Women's WORLD (India)**



ISBN: 81-88965-62-6



Cover design: PealiDezine

*We have made every effort to contact all poets and translators for permission to use their poems in this anthology. However, if some have been omitted please do inform us and we will rectify this in the next edition.*

# CONTENTS

# ACKNOWLEDGEMENTS

Grateful thanks are due, first and most importantly, to all the poets in this anthology for allowing us to include their poems in it, and to many of them for participating in our 10 workshops on gender-based censorship in India, between 1999–2006.

In particular, and in addition, we'd like to say a big thank you to Arlene Zide for help in locating and translating some truly wonderful Hindi poems for us; to Mangai and Mini Sukumar for help with Tamil and Malayalam poets; to Sampurna Chattarji for directing us to an anthology of Marathi poetry; to Prathibha Nandakumar for help with poems from Kannada; to K. Satchidanandan for his note on Rose Mary; to Subashree Krishnaswamy and K. Srilata for so generously agreeing to translate poems from Tamil, at very short notice; to Sudeep Sen for introducing us to Mithu Sen's poetry; to *the little magazine* and Antara Dev Sen for Nabaneeta Dev Sen's poems.

Finally, our heartfelt gratitude to Keki Daruwalla for his Foreword, and for being so spontaneously supportive of our effort.

# PREFACE

Between 1999 and 2006, a most unusual and unique series of workshops, with over 200 women writers in ten major regional languages, were held in different cities across the country. This was an initiative of Women's WORLD (India), a free-speech network of writers, literary critics and some editors, that is concerned with women's writing and the gendered nature of censorship. Our women and censorship project evolved from, and is part of, Women's World Organisation for Rights, Literature and Development, a network that seeks to catalyse global feminist work on the right to free expression.

What is it that connects women to writing? And what is it that defines and determines the contours of that writing? What are the limits of the freedom that women are allowed in self-expression? Is a poem or a short story like an exotic sweet, or a neatly embroidered handwork, or a well-trained voice, to be displayed on occasion as a sign of feminine accomplishment? Marked by measured cadences and neatly drawn lines—never flamboyant, never demanding attention, just gently drawing praise with modest, womanly grace. What do women write? What is it they cannot write about? Who reads them? Who publishes them? Are some languages more privileged than others? Some genres more accessible?

These were the questions and confusions that haunted us during and after our workshops in Urdu, Telugu, Marathi, Malayalam, Hindi, Gujarati, Kannada, Bangla, English and

Tamil, that brought up new issues and allowed fresh insights into the nature of censorship that women face. The thread that ran through most of them was disconnection: the disconnect between what women said and what they wrote; between their spoken words and their silences; between their husbands' and fathers' apparent encouragement and support, and their explicit, disapproving silence when a norm was violated. Between women as the subject-matter of writing, and women as subjects and writers. Between language, literature and social movements, and the emergence of women's voices. Between language and gender, gender and genre.

The primary purpose of these interactions was to collectively determine whether or not female creative writers in India face any form of censorship (direct or indirect) from any quarter: the state, the market, community leaders, society at large, families, even themselves. We wished to explore the idea that gender-based censorship, embedded in a range of social and cultural mechanisms that invalidate women's experience and exclude them from political discourse, is often far more pervasive and far more difficult to confront than official suppression. We wanted to examine how critical the silencing of women, and the use of systematic force — direct or indirect — to ensure that silence, is to the maintenance and perpetuation of patriarchal power.

The range and depth of discussions, and the sharing of experiences during these workshops, were astonishing and gratifying in their richness and complexity. Once begun it was difficult to stop the flow, to disentangle the personal from the familial; from the social and cultural; and indeed, from the political. Impossible not to take caste and community into account when talking about literature and language; or about religion and sexuality. Abundantly clear, when discussing the novel, short story or poem that women's choice of genre is so often determined by time and space, by the constraints of domesticity, by a life of repeated interruption.

Towards the end of this initial phase of our project, we published two volumes of in-depth interviews with 35 of our participating writers: *Storylines: Conversations with Women Writers* in 2003, and *Just Between Us: Women Speak about their Writing* in 2004. This anthology is an attempt to present a selection of poems from the ten languages of our workshops by the poets in our group, with the addition of a few who were unable to attend for one reason or another. It goes without saying that the selection is subjective; that we were constrained by the difficulty of getting satisfactory translations; that some languages are better represented than others; that no single volume can possibly do justice to the vast amount of poetry written by women in India.

We plead guilty to all these; but hope that what is offered here will be tempting enough, and satisfying enough, to encourage the translation and publication of many more poets and many more volumes, slim or otherwise, of which this is just the beginning.

AMMU JOSEPH
VASANTH KANNABIRAN
RITU MENON
VOLGA
WOMEN'S WORLD (INDIA)

# FOREWORD

A genuinely fine poetry volume in several Indian languages casts its own special spell on the reader. Just watching each language sail into such an anthology with its ballast—its local symbols, conventions, its own particular way of articulating a feeling—is fascinating. Take Urdu for instance, the victim of deliberate neglect over the last 60 years in India. Jameela Nishat writes for the poet Vali Dakhani, whose grave was razed and a road built over it during the Gujarat riots of 2002.

> Wandering in the body's city
> the wounded man
> lay at the heart's threshold
> He knew
> that the cheek too is a garden
> but its fragrance is beyond the mind's reach

You won't find such lines in other languages—the cheek as garden, or lying down 'at the heart's threshold'. Later we have 'Hands raised in prayer/ Cut down/ The rosary of pearly tears/ Now a chain of iron links.' This is the way much, or at least a part, of Urdu poetry is written, the emotional tempo raised, the lamentation shrill (as in Arabic and Persian) and the symbolism stark. Another poem of hers, again on the killings in Gujarat, starts with the lines 'The red of my palms/ Wasn't henna but blood'. Symbolism couldn't be more obvious or more hard-hitting.

Sometimes liberty moves towards the edge of license. Gagan Gill, the fine Hindi poet, starts off a poem with, 'In the days of the dead, sometimes our mothers would descend from the sky.' One can see what she's getting at; the mothers worrying over the food, the indifferent fathers descending later. Yet the libations in the end are only offered to the fathers. The point is, does one need this rain of mothers and fathers to make this point? These descents from the sky and 'the days of the dead' could leave the reader uneasy. Similarly, Nishat states 'Rising one by one the corpses set out/ bathed in the light of the western moon…' Couldn't we do without the corpses marching away or parents drizzling from the heavens? But this is panache, liberty, style, whatever you call it, that Indian language poetry gives itself over to at times.

Yet, mixed with all this is beautiful poetry. Here is Anamika writing 'Read us carefully / one word at a time' and later, 'Look at us with yearning/ as, shivering, you would look at a fire/ out of reach.'

> Listen to us
> as you would the soundless void
> and try to understand, slowly,
>         a language newly learned.

The Tamil poems included here are staggeringly hard-hitting. Kutti Revathy's 'Not for Sale' says:

> Unable to dissolve the poverty line ever
> I decided to sell my breasts.

Such lines don't just hit you in the gut, they alter your perceptions, the way you look at the world. (And I may be forgiven for thinking all the time that such lines would never be encountered in poetry from the West.) In another poem of hers one comes across a poignant juxtaposition. As two people cut a dead tree, 'One/ Thought of his father/ On his deathbed; The other/ Ashamed, recalled his wife's face/ Twisted with tears after having sex.' This strain runs through the book, the power the male exercises, and the surrender to his whims and his libido. The Tamil poet, Salma, tells her husband in her poem, 'Midnight' that after her deliveries her 'Bloated body/ And stretch-marked stomach / Disgust you.'

The volume obviously contains poems on children (Gauri Deshpande), poems on mothers (Ilampirai), poems on birth and deliveries, a searing poem by Salma on her uterus being removed after an operation. Neglect, and cruelty from the inconsiderate male implicit in such neglect, has an abiding presence in the volume, and why not? Anamika, the Hindi poet, tells us that a man's heart is a salt mountain. She also says in her poem, 'Women',

> They read us
>             casually
> like one reads the torn pages
> of a child's notebook
> before it is made into paper-cones.

Bilqees Zefirul Hasan, the Urdu poet, has a narrative poem where the au pair, Dhaniya, tells the mistress that her husband came back every night, 'dead drunk' and beat her up. Never gave her any money to spend. She left him. The mistress is unhappy and tells her, 'you shouldn't have left your husband and walked away'. The pathos, of course, lies in such surrender, and the poets don't mince their words telling us about them. Vijayalakshmi (Malayalam) says in the poem, 'The Beast Trainer', 'My body tires/ before his grimace/ I bow, how can I not/ salute his fearsome grace.' Later in the same poem she adds, 'Fear, fear alone, fills/ my slavish heart.'

Obviously one can't pigeonhole such a vast variety of excellent poetry. One also comes across great assurance. Rose Mary, the Malayalam poet, writes

> Like one emperor to another,
> like one friend to another,
> come to me
> as an equal.
> Like a flute
> pursuing the tune,
> like the question
> seeking its answer
> may your steps be
> as light
> and as carefree . . .

This anthology is intense and modern, razor-sharp and feminist. (Anything feminist is razor-sharp, if you ask me. It wouldn't be feminist otherwise.) Only now and then is there a throwback, for instance in Savithri Rajeevan's Malayalam poem on Krishna—the Mirabai strain should not be altogether lost to the feminine muse.

Much of the poetry in the book is about protest. Writing in Telugu, Shahajahana attacks the veil, the way Imtiaz Dharker did in an entire book.

> How many dreams are slaughtered
> behind each veil
> how many desires
> how many hopes
> lie smashed behind dark veils
> where life is imprisoned behind a veil
> where mighty banyans of mad orthodoxy flourish
> stamping women down . . .

Lest we get the idea that the poetry in this volume is all about victimhood or male-bashing, that impression needs to be corrected. We have here sensual poems like 'Jugal Bandhi' by Ghantasala Nirmala (Telugu) that ripple over the page, two fish poems by Gagan Gill, a splendid parable by Rajee Seth on the window watching the cosmos, while the sky can never take in the window's vision pouring out through the opening. Amrita Bharati has a poignant poem on desert as memory or memory as desert, and there is also a lovely river poem by Mamta Sagar in Kannada.

A word about poets writing in English is necessary, because women poets are in the vanguard of English poetry in India. Imtiaz Dharkar, Arundhati Subramaniam, Rukmini Bhaya Nair and Meena Alexander are the leading lights of English poetry in the country today. The older poets, Gauri Deshpande and Kamala Das (both tragically no longer with us) may at times talk of ungrateful children or unloving and unfaithful men but the younger poets, possibly because of their backgrounds, are not defensive. Deshpande even attacks Orpheus for looking back, 'trying to ascertain the nature of faith' of Eurydice, even though she would have escorted him from Hades into light. Kamala Das's older poems like 'Introduction' may talk of unrequited love, but she has other long magisterial poems in this volume.

Though Mamang Dai can write about the sorrows of women, and Rukmini Bhaya Nair may equate a woman with a comma or a semi-colon, by and large they tackle other subjects, and their interests are diverse. Ancestors become a focal point with some. Both Kamala Das and Meena Alexander write lovingly on mothers and even great-grandmothers. Meena Alexander has some searing poems on Gujarat where she questions Gandhi about the riots in 2002. (Gujarat has turned into a salt lick for poets.)

The Gargi poem, a minor classic by Rukmini Bhaya Nair, is missing, but her Sappho poem, slightly long drawn, is around. She tells us in 'Reasons' that 'in the end a woman writes as/ Nature dictates'. The poem does talk of

> Loneliness
>         Like dry strokes fading
> In the inkwells of her heart
>         A woman

Writes her epitaph
With slow regret

Menka Shivdasani in her poem 'Epitaph' writes that when she holds her pain,

That's when the poem writes itself
like an epitaph.

The Bengali section is very powerful. Mandakranta Sen starts her poem 'The Witch' with the lines

One who writes poetry in the middle of the night
With her hair undone is a witch.
After everyone's asleep, she soaks in clear moonlight
On netherworld's roof . . .

She has a fine poem on the Nature Goddess and a wild one on Lesbos, which starts:

Blood on her face, chest; blood between her legs—
This wild smell of blood has made me crave and beg.

Nabaneeta Dev Sen has some fine poems, especially the one on Calcutta ('Return of the Dead'). Her poems here are light of step—'The heart folds up its tent and steps out into the road.' Only in patches does she strike a pensive note:

should I call it love
should I call it longing
inside my head these dark forests
in my heart these sixty miles of empty highway

desolate
jamming my jaws, rocks
choking my throat, sand dunes
roaring inside my head, cascades . . .

'Sand dunes', and later 'cascades' coming in after 'dark forests' could leave some readers uneasy. We are not in the habit of carrying one metaphor forward—in this case the one relating to 'dark forests'.

Saroop Dhruv (Gujarati), whose poem 'I' starts with the line 'I am a resolution to survive', asserts later 'Here I am, as strong as a foundation / A root, a base; like grammar.' And she has a strong poem on Taslima Nasrin. Manisha Joshi's poems deal lovingly with birds—flamingoes, cranes and the mythical phoenix – and bring nature to your doorstep.

The Marathi poets skewer the male, good and proper. (Not that the males don't deserve it.) Pradnya Lokhande traces the heritage of her 'gender's simmering'; Kavita Mahajan is all satire when she says her own flesh is as soft as sunflower petals 'Showing off openly/ The seductive seeds.' Like the other Marathi poets here, she can be wickedly delightful as she tells us that

Women with masters
Avoid
Women without masters

But even as they put on their mangalsutra and 'adjust their kumkum' they glance stealthily at the independent ones without masters. In a poem on Dali's painting Malika Amar

Sheikh (Marathi) does to poetry what Dali did to painting—turns it on its head. 'What is behind that huge eyelid?/ A watch/ A moment/ a silence/ Or a dead tear?' Her poem 'Metropolis' starts with the lines, 'A total woman/ Complete with a womb' and then asks, 'Is bed an answer to all the questions?' After sex, the male is not even aware whether

> The one sleeping next to you
> Is a woman or graveyard or dung.

Now you can't get more scathing than that, can you? But there is great humour here, too, for when the male crosses the Atlantic

> . . . you land on their nipples
> And cry, 'America, America! Eureka, eureka...'

After this, what is there left to say?

For thousands of years women have been assiduously keeping alive the flame of poetry in us through their oral narratives. Not just poetry but our dormant, if not moribund, imaginations were lit up through these narratives, which were both memorised and also in a way reinvented, as they passed from mouth to mouth. They have been excluded from the written word for far too long, though evidence even of the written word from them goes back two thousand years. Meanwhile, we can only look at any anthology which bares the female psyche with such sensitivity, in humility and awe.

Delhi, 2009 KEKI N. DARUWALLA

# URDU

## JAMEELA NISHAT

### *For Vali*

Wandering in the body's city
the wounded man
lay at the heart's threshold
He knew
that the cheek too is a garden
but its fragrance is beyond the mind's reach
Where he stood
That place is ruined
That place is Ahmedabad
He remembers
That blood-soaked sheet twined with burning hair
Hands raised in prayer
Cut down
The rosary of pearly tears
Now a chain of iron links
Lips parted
Tongue parched
The wounded man lies at the crossroads
On his palm is a lit lamp
Which will light
every body and soul
See it is a woman's soul that rises
                    from Vali the poet's grave

*Translated by Hoshang Merchant*

### *The red of my palms / Wasn't henna but blood*

The red of my palms
Wasn't henna but blood
One cry from my heart
Burnt this earth to cinders
You smouldered / I turned air
And flowed your way
What did I know which way
The dew on my grass
Shone by your sight
Becoming a rainbow by light
Becoming honey at night
Was it a dream behind my eyes
Or a mirage made of your sighs
All I did was ponder this
I went nowhere
Neither here nor there
The one my sight searches
What do I know where she is
Come, let us smash all riddles
Come, let us make a new world
And search out new roads
New dreams, new loves
New feelings, new music
All of us queens and fairies
All stories, love-stories

*Translated by Hoshang Merchant*

## *Untitled*

Rising one by one the corpses set out
bathed in the light of the western moon
The bones washed away
The air is filled with a new chemistry
breaking a fresh star with each footstep
There can be no more compromise
Death cannot reign thus any more
Bombs unceasingly made and scattered across the earth
People dying and rising from graveyards
Are you at peace having sold the country?
The rivers afloat with our corpses
The streets steeled with spilt blood
Do you not see the corpses wherever you turn?
Dealing with a python
Sifting and selling each hope one by one
You sold the Indian Ocean and the Arabian Sea
Selling your country
How are you at peace?
from the shore the fisherfolk speak.
our corpses fill the ocean
The worn-out bones rising and tossed by the waves.
We dart through the ocean like currents
Who can escape the fisherman's net?
What if you sell our uranium? Hiroshima and Nagasaki can
return again.
Slumber is deep but people cannot sleep

All are innocent but none ignorant
no not drunk nor forgetful
Again Bhopal speaks
We are dead no one could kill us
Crippled we walked to Delhi
There can be no more compromise.

*Translated by Hoshang Merchant*

## *For Mazhar Mehdi, Poet (d. 2009)*

No poems    No words
No feeling
Nothing
Emotions caught in webs of philosophy
Within my bowels seep poisons to kill poison
A maelstorm of medicines
In a hospital white-clad men
                walk around me

Pain floods in
Every nerve pulls every minute
Breaths are screams
The entire body trembles
2009
for thousands of years has genuflected
                at the threshold of touch
Prayers on my lips
My finger-tips itch

Stuck in my body
are bottles
Red—white
Light
What is this cure
That makes hands raised in prayer
tremble
My tongue a bed of nails
cuts into my conscience
In a white room    Clad in pure white
Amid clean, transparent mirrors I lie
Every emotion buried in those mirrors within mirrors

*Translated by Hoshang Merchant*

## BILQEES ZEFIRUL HASAN

### *Four Nazms*

### *Dignity*

"Bibi Sahab, my husband
would come home every night, deadly drunk. Then he
would batter me.
He wouldn't let me spend even a cent from his earnings.
How could I live with such a man? I left him,
left the village and came to the city.

Now I work in rich people's homes, such as you,
I earn for myself and live by my labour.
What good is the vermillion in the hair that adorns, but like
a wound?"

Now how could the Bibi Sahab explain to Dhaniya
that her story wasn't one of a kind
that she too endures something similar,
day after day, night after night.

But, unluckily, she isn't Dhaniya. She is Bibi Sahab.
And this status has been given to her as a reward by her
husband.

(One who has no status of one's own must live on charity
alone.)

The dignity she attains by living with her husband:
Can a woman hope to find it elsewhere? Anywhere?

Feeling the gash on her forehead as she speaks,
"Dhaniya, you shouldn't have left your husband and walked
away."

Self- respect *is something*; but how should Dhaniya make
Bibi Sahab understand this?

*Translated by Mehr Afshan Farooqi*

## *Will You Be My Friend?*

If one makes up one's mind to do something, anything is
possible.
Indeed, I too can be unfaithful,
Flirtatious—
Scorn, sarcasm, unkind remarks, all of this!
These nuggets from you —I can throw them right back in
your face.

Don't think I am naïve or weak.
If one makes up one's mind to do something, anything is
possible.
But what will I get? — Causing pain
doesn't make me happy—I don't like it.

Why should I spend my energies foolishly?

I am your 'better half' after all!
If I come down to your level I will fall from my place.
My children's foreheads bear your name.
I have to keep it glowing—
What lengths you have gone to humiliate me.
Try being friends, just once.
It won't be a bad deal—I promise
Say? Will you be my friend?

*Translated by Mehr Afshan Farooqi*

## *Some Poems: Craving Indulgence*

Desires! If they could become horses, even so,
how can beggars ride on them?
Saddle, spurs, reins are the property
of the rider who wields the whip.
With what authority can those who crawl on the ground
use them?
They don't have
the courtyards, the backyards where
these horses can be harnessed.

*ii*

Velvet beetles of the rainy months.
Nestled in the lap
of the lushness that follows the downpours
in which clouds are emptied
Like rubies, so red, so shiny, luminous.

If you do find one,
I pray you, please don't touch;
For then they become motionless, numb.

*iii*
Scattering a rainbow of bright colours, innocent,
never staying long at any place.
Hot in pursuit, racing around
breathless, running fast, so fast,
panting, hearts thumping loudly.
Then quiet; disappointment writ in eyes,
The butterfly flies off, most times.
Who has touched a rainbow?

*Translated by Mehr Afshan Farooqi*

## *Untitled Nazm*

I doubt if one can find oneself,
but I suppose there is nothing wrong in trying.
They say—if you find yourself, you find God.
Anyway, having a nice pursuit
to while away idle time is not bad at all.
There isn't a better pastime for leisure than this.
But resist straying here and there.
Stop yourself from wandering in the deserts, in the
wildernesses.
Lying somewhere in a corner of every busy family home
there is also a garden.

You can find yours by staying where you are.
Random wanderings can be extremely dangerous.
You can lose yourself.

Unfortunately I am a woman—not bad looking either
fairly intelligent as well—so this danger
increases a million times.

*Translated by Mehr Afshan Farooqi*

# ENGLISH

## GAURI DESHPANDE

### *The Female of the Species*

Sometimes you want to talk
about love and despair
and the ungratefulness of children.
A man is no use whatever then.
You want then your mother
or sister
or the girl with whom you went through school,
and your first love, and her
first child—a girl—
and your second.
You sit with them and talk
She sews and you sit and sip
and speak of the rate of rice
and the price of tea
and the scarcity of cheese.
You both know that you've spoken
of love and despair and ungrateful children.

### *The Habit*

The puppy-dog died
And I cried my heart out.
There, there, they said,
Poor baby, they said,

You'll get over it,
You'll get used to it.
(Dying puppy-dogs, they meant.)

When I grew up
I lost an arm
a friend, a child, a shade
And they were right.

I got over it
I got used to it
All dying and my living.

Now when I see him crossing a street
to me, coming swiftly
How am I going to get used to him,
It's the first time
And I've had no time.

## *Prometheus and Orpheus*

To cold and fixed certainty —
my life — you brought the intensity
of your fire.
For this gift I wonder,
will you be fixed to the vast
and arid immobility
where ever-gnawing unfulfilment

shall eat away
your core of joy?

~ ~ ~

If only you hadn't turned
she'd have followed you
to the gates of Hades
and into sunlight;
but trying to ascertain the nature of faith
you glimpse only
her retreating shade.

## *Between Births*

This was born in April
the month of rebirth
and this in September
the beginning of death
I span my life between
the mango's blossoming
and the winter-jasmine
and conclude as the rain lets up
early before fulfilling the green
promises, that this shall be
a year of drought

## *Poems on a Lost Love*

1

When you left me lying
in you-smelling warmth
to course slowly
along deserted roads
I hated the cold air
drying my sweat on your hands
and driving my thought
from your tired thigh
which will be astonished tomorrow
to find on it the blue-black
and urgent mark.

2

The alchemy of my blood
that stained and matted your belly-hair
has converted you magically
and made us the same;
each the other's branded secret self
bejewelled and bright red
in a fellowship of blood.

3

I am earth.
Vast deep and black
and I receive
the first rain

sweet, generous,
lashing, throbbing;
its smell forever in my blood
its imprint deep
within my quick.
Yellow daisies burst out
on my breast and thigh
at its every touch.

4
I've met your eyes across strangers' speech
and have seen the flickering memories
of long journeys
beyond confines
of need and desire
and have thrilled shivering to think
of what you think
alone in your sleep,
have clenched my teeth to keep within
the cry, deep, till we should meet
and you unlock and smother it
with your lips.

5
When our bodies' rhythm
requires concentration
and our hands slip
slick with sweat and lost

in gasps
then your fist tells
my hair in a jerky grip
to contain and communicate
our joyous exhaustion;
the forgotten mouths
coming together at last
to taste the smiles.

6
When your lips softened under mine
and your hands stilled over my shoulder-blades
I knew it was time to draw apart
yet didn't, for you breathed me in
like a man in heavy sleep
and didn't say anything.

## *Workaday Women*

1
In a city
there are six long mondays
when you spend your mornings
jammed up against women
sour-smelling from sweat,
perfume, talcum, soap;
each bracing to face the files,
machines, pencils, pupils, people,
sights, yells, lunches, delays.

And evenings they are packed more dense
grimy with weariness.
Their eyes are vacant and they don't push
even to get off the train.

2
The skin will thicken, toughen,
protect you from seeing the tailless cat, his forepaw torn;
the man with a gash from ear to ear, sewn
with forty-seven stitches;
and long ditches of water
bordered by mounds of filth;
of course, small children
whose sight is agony.
On six long mondays you
are pushed, pulled, dully
stared at, thick-opaque.

3
And the too-solid flesh
will refuse
when he demands that it melt
at a saturday-touch.
You have not been protected after all
from women men children cats.

## KAMALA DAS

### *An Introduction*

I don't know politics but I know the names
Of those in power, and can repeat them like
Days of the week, or names of months,
beginning with Nehru.
I am Indian, very brown, born in Malabar,
I speak three languages, write in
Two, dream in one. Don't write in English, they said,
English is not your mother-tongue. Why not leave
Me alone, critics, friends, visiting cousins,
Every one of you? Why not let me speak in
Any language I like? The language I speak
Becomes mine, mine alone. It is half English, half
Indian, funny perhaps, but it is honest.
It is as human as I am human, don't
You see? It voices my joys, my longings, my
Hopes, and it is useful to me as cawing
Is to crows or roaring to the lions, it
Is human speech, the speech of the mind that is
Here and not there, a mind that sees, that hears and
Is aware. Not the deaf, blind speech
Of trees in storm or of monsoon clouds or of rain or the
Incoherent mutterings of the blazing
Funeral pyre.

I was child, and later they
Told me I grew, for I became tall, my limbs
Swelled and one or two places sprouted hair. When
I asked for love, not knowing what else to ask
For, he drew a youth of sixteen into the
Bedroom and closed the door. He did not beat me
But my sad woman-body felt so beaten.
The weight of my breasts and womb crushed me. I shrank
Pitifully. Then ...
I wore a shirt and my
Brother's trousers, cut my hair short and ignored
My womanliness. Dress in saris, be girl
Be wife, they said. Be embroiderer, be cook,
Belong, cried the categorisers. Don't sit
On walls or peep in through our lace-draped windows.
Be Amy, or be Kamala. Or, better
Still, be Madhavikutty. It is time to
Choose a name, a role. Don't play pretending games.
Don't play at schizophrenia or be a
Nympho. Don't cry embarrassingly loud when
Jilted in love ...

I met a man, loved him. Call
Him not by any name, he is every man
Who wants a woman, just as I am every
Woman who seeks love. In him the hungry haste
Of rivers, in me the ocean's tireless
Waiting. Who are you, I ask each and every one,

The answer is, it is I. Anywhere and
Everywhere, I see the one who calls himself
If in this world, he is tightly packed liked the
Sword in its sheath. It is I who drink lonely
Drinks at twelve, midnight, in hotels of strange towns,
It is I who laugh, it is I who make love
And then, feel shame, it is I who lies dying
With a rattle in my throat. I am sinner,
I am saint. I am the beloved and the
Betrayed. I have no joys which are not yours, no
Aches which are not yours. I too call myself I.

## *Composition*

Ultimately,
I have come face to face with the sea.
In the beginning
the sea was only the wind's
ceaseless whisper in a shell.
But, lying beside my grandmother,
quite often I thought
that surf breaking on the shore,
The sea was only two miles away.
That was long ago.
Before the skin
intent on survival
learnt lessons of self-betrayal.
Before the red house that had
stood for innocence

crumbled
and the old woman died,
lying for the three months
paralysed,
while the thieving ants climbed her hands
and ate the cuticle.

Perhaps my innocence is not
all that lost
if the stone still endures
and pieces of mortar lie scattered
in the field.
It may be
that in my heart
I have replaced love with guilt
and discovered
that both love and hate are
involvements.
But this only signifies growth
and growth is natural.
The tragedy of life
is not death but growth,
the child growing into adult
and growing out of needs
discovering
that the old have black- rimmed nails
and scalps that emanate
a sweet mouldy smell.

In the years that followed
I was busy growing
I had then
no time at all for the sea.
But
there was off and on a seascape
in my dreams,
and the water sloshing up
and sliding down.

When I got married
my husband said
You may have freedom
as much as you want.
My soul balked at this diet of ash.
Freedom became my dancing shoe
How well I danced
and danced without rest
until the shoes turned grimy on my feet
and I began to have doubts.
I asked my husband,
am I hetero
am I lesbian
or am I just plain frigid?
He only laughed.
For such questions
there are probably no answers
or else
the answers must emerge

from within.
I have lost my best friend
to a middle-aged queer,
The lesbians hiss their love at me.
Love
I no longer need,
with tenderness I am most content
I have learnt that friendship
cannot endure
that blood-ties do not satisfy
and so
with every interesting man I meet
be it
a curious editor,
or poet with a skin yellowed
like antique paper
a skin older than Jesus Christ
I must
most deliberately
whip up a froth of desire
a passion to suit the occasion.
I must let my mind striptease
I must extrude
autobiography.
The only secrets I always
withhold
are that I am so alone
and that I miss my grandmother.

Reader,
you may say
now here is a girl with vast
sexual hungers
a bitch after my own heart.
But,
I am not yours for the asking.
Grovel at my feet,
remove your monkey-suits and dance,
sing Erato Erato Erato,
Yet I shall be indifferent.
Not because of morality
but because
I do not feel the need.
But why worry?
What I am able to give
is only what your wife is qualified
to give.
We are all alike,
we women,
in our wrappings of hairless skin.
All skeletons are alike,
only the souls vary
that hide somewhere between the flesh
and the bone.
Skin a human being and he will
still breathe.
Starve a person, break his flesh
until he is reduced

to skin and bone,
and yet he will live
with attention.
But stripped of a skin and flesh
the skeleton is dead
and most indifferent to the soul.

When I was home on vacation
some thirteen years ago
my grandmother asked me to spend
one night
in the old family home.
We shall talk, she said,
darling,
we shall talk all night,
and in the evening
she kept a lighted lantern
on the window-still
and sat up waiting for me.
The house was four hundred years old
its rafters shook in the wind.
Those who thought my life precious,
cried
do not go there,
we shall have no peace
with you sleeping under that
tottering roof.
My grandmother's lamp burned
all night

on the window-still.
I know it is no use regretting now
or feeling ashamed.
I also know that by confessing
by peeling off my layers
I reach closer to the soul
and
to the bone's
supreme indifference.

Only those who like to listen,
listen.
What I narrate are the ordinary
events of an
ordinary life.

My first school-house
is now a brothel,
and
the ladies sun themselves on the lawn
in the afternoons
with their graying hair
newly washed,
left undyed.
Who can say, looking at them,
that they are toys
fit for the roaring nights ?
There must be something symbolic here,

but I do not
remember what.
I have gathered a few morals too
picking them
like wild flowers
on my way.
Husbands and wives,
here is my advice to you.
Obey each other's crazy commands,
ignore the sane.
Turn your home into a merry
dog-house,
marriage is meant to be all this
anyway,
being arranged in
most humorous heaven.
I have reached the age at which
one forgives all.
I am ready to forgive friends
their loving,
forgive those who ruined friendships
and those who forgave
and stayed on to love.
But I shall give a lot to get
one of my foes today
for a quiet picnic
somewhere.
Not having met for ages

we shall have so much to say,
But
Seriously. I must wake up,
come alive.
I tell myself
and all of you
who scan the mirror for that white
gleam in the hair,
fall in love,
fall in love with an unsuitable
person
fling yourself at him
like a moth on a flame.
Let there be despair in every move.
Excavate
Deep deep pain.
To be frank,
I have failed.
I feel my age and my
uselessness.
All I want now
is to take a long walk
into the sea
and lie there, resting,
completely uninvolved.

But,
rest is only a childish whim,

a minor hunger.
Greater hungers lurk
at the basement of the sea.
Ultimately
I will feed only the hunger
to feed other hungers,
that basic one.
To crumble,
to dissolve
and to retain in other things
the potent fragments
of oneself.
The ultimate discovery will be
that we are immortal,
the only things mortal being
systems and arrangements,
even our pains continuing
in the devourers who constitute
the world. Even
oft repeated moves
of every scattered cell
will give no power
to escape
from cages of involvement.
I must linger on,
trapped in immortality,
my only freedom being
the freedom to
discompose.

## *Blood*

When we were children
My brother and I
And always playing on the sands
Drawing birds and animals
Our great-grandmother said one day,
You see this house of ours
Now three hundred years old,
It's falling to little bits
Before our very eyes
The walls are cracked and torn
And moistened by rain,
The tiles have fallen here and there
The windows whine and groan
And every night
The rats come out of holes
And scamper past our doors.
The snake-shrine is dark with weeds
And all the snake-gods in the shrine
Have lichen on their hoods.
O, it hurts me she cried,
Wiping a reddened eye
For I love this house, it hurts me much
To watch it die.

When I grow old, I said,
And very very rich

I shall rebuild the fallen walls
And make new this ancient house.

My grandmother
Touched my cheeks and smiled.
She was really simple,
Fed on God for years
All her feasts were monotonous
For the only dish was always God
And the rest mere condiments.
She told us how she rode her elephant
When she was ten or eleven
Every Monday without fail
To the Shiva shrine
And back home again
And told us of the jewel-box
And the brocade from the north
And the perfumes and the oils
And the sandal for her breasts
And her marriage to a prince
Who loved her deeply for a lovely short year
 and died of fever, in her arms.
She told us
That we had the oldest blood
My brother and she and I
The oldest blood in the world
A blood thin and clear and fine
While in the veins of the always poor

And in the veins
Of the new- rich men
Flowed a blood thick as gruel
And muddy as a ditch.
Finally she lay dying
In her eighty-sixth year
A woman wearied by compromise
Her legs quilted with arthritis
And with only a hard cough
For comfort.
I looked deep into her eyes
Her poor bleary eyes
And prayed that she would not grieve
So much about the house.
I had learnt by then
Most lessons of defeat,
Had found out that to grow rich
Was a difficult feat.
The house was crouching
On its elbows then.
It looked that night in the pallid moon
So grotesque and alive.
When they burnt my grandmother
Over logs of the mango tree
I looked once at the house
And then again and again
For I thought I saw the windows close
Like the closing of the eyes

I thought I heard the pillars groan
and the dark rooms heave a sigh.

I set forth again
For other towns,
Left the house with the shrine
And the sands
And the flowering shrubs
And the wide rabid mouth of the Arabian Sea.

I know the rats are running now
Across the darkened halls
They do not fear the dead.
I know the white ants have reached my home
And have raised on walls
Strange totems of burial.
At night, in stillness,
From every town I live in
I hear the rattle of its death
The noise of rafters creaking
And the windows' whine.
I have let you down
Old house, I seek forgiveness
O mother's mother's mother
I have plucked your soul
Like a pip from a fruit
And have flung it into your pyre
Call me callous

Call me selfish
But do not blame my blood
So thin, so clear, so fine
The oldest blood in the world
That remembers as it flows
All the gems and all the gold
And all the perfumes and all the oils
And the stately
Elephant ride.

## *Glass*

I went to him for half an hour
As pure woman, pure misery
Fragile glass, breaking
Crumbling . . .
The house was silent in the heat
Only the old rafters creaking
He drew me to him
Rudely
With a lover's haste, an armful
Of splinters designed to hurt and
Pregnant with pain. Why
Did I
Not cry then, broken glass, beware?
Why did I not tell him them that
I no longer care
Whom I
Hurt with love and often without?

With a cheap toy's indifference
I enter others'
Lives and
Make of every trap of lust
A temporary home. On me, their
Strumming fingers may
Revive
The fond melodies of a past
I give a wrapping to their dreams,
A woman-voice
And a
Woman-smell. I do not bother
To tell: I've misplaced a father
Somewhere, and I look
For him now everywhere.

## *Convicts*

There was a time when our lusts were
Like multicoloured flags of no
Particular country. We lay
On the bed, glassy-eyed, fatigued, just
The toys dead children leave behind,
And we asked each other, what is
The use, what is the bloody use ?
That was the only kind of love,
This hacking at each other's parts
Like convicts hacking, breaking clods
At noon. We were earth under hot

Sun. There was a burning in our
Veins and the cool mountain nights did
Nothing to lessen heat. When he
And I were one, we were neither
Male or female. There were no more
Words left, all words lay imprisoned
In the ageing arms of night. In
Darkness we grew as in silence
We sang, each note rising out of
Sea, out of wind, out of earth and
Out of each sad night like an ache.

## *My Grandmother's House*

There is a house now far away where once
I received love. That woman died,
The house withdrew into silence, snakes moved
Among books. I was then too young
To read, and my blood turned cold like the moon
How often I think of going
There, to peer through blind eyes of windows or
Just listen to the frozen air
Or in wild despair, pick an armful of
Darkness to bring it here to lie
Behind my bedroom door like a brooding
Dog ... you cannot believe, darling,
Can you, that I lived in such a house and
Was proud, and loved ... I who have lost

My way and beg now at strangers' doors to
Receive love, at least in small change?

## *The Stone Age*

Fond husband, ancient settler in the mind,
Old fat spider, weaving webs of bewilderment,
Be kind. You turn me into a bird of stone, a granite
Dove, you build round me a shabby drawing room,
And stroke my pitted face absent-mindedly while
You read. With loud talk you bruise my pre-morning sleep,
You stick a finger into my dreaming eye. And
Yet, on daydreams, strong men cast their shadows, they sink
Like white suns in the swell of my Dravidian blood,
Secretly flow the drains beneath sacred cities.
When you leave, I drive my blue battered car
Along the bluer sea. I run up the forty
Noisy steps to knock at another's door.
Through peep-holes, the neighbours watch,
They watch me come
And go like rain. Ask me, everybody, ask me
What he sees in me, ask me why he is called a lion,
A libertine, ask me the flavour of his
Mouth, ask me why his hand sways like a hooded snake
Before it clasps my pubis. Ask me why like
A great tree felled, he slumps against my breasts
And sleeps. Ask me why life is short and love is
Shorter still, ask me what is bliss and what its price . . .

## MEENA ALEXANDER

### *Rites of Sense*

In twilight as she lies on a mat
I rub my mother's feet with jasmine oil
touch callouses under skin,
joints upholding that fraught original thing—
bone, gristle, skin, all that makes her mine.
All day she swabbed urine from the floor,
father's legs so weak he clung to the rosewood bed.
She rinsed soiled cloths, hung them out to dry
on a coir rope by a vine, its passion fruit
clumsy with age, dangling.

She lies on a mat, a poor thing beached,
belly slack, soles crossed, sari damp and white.
I kneel in darkness at her side,
her oldest child returned for a few weeks
at summer's height.
She murmurs my name
asks in Malayalam *Why is light so hot?*

Beyond her spine I catch a candle glisten.
The door's a frame for something
I'm too scared to name:
a child, against a white wall,
hands jammed to her teeth, lips torn
breath staggering its hoarse silence.

All night my voice laced through dreams
tiny eyelets for the smoke
*Amma, I am burning!*
I'm a voice slit from sound,
just snitches of blood, loopholes of sweat,
a sack of flesh you shut me in.

What words of passage to that unlit place?
What rites of sense?

Amma, I am dreaming myself into your body.
It is the end of everything.
Your pillow stained with white
tosses as a wave might
on our southern shore.

Will you lay your cheek against mine?
Bless my bent head?

You washed me once, gave me suck,
made me live in your father's house
taught me to wake at dawn,
sweep the threshold clean of blood-red leaves.
Showed me a patch of earth dug with your hands
where sweet beans grow coiled and raw.

Taught me to fire a copper pan,
starch and fold a sari, raise a rusty needle,

stitch my woman's breath
into the mute amazement of sentences.

## *Torn Grass*

Childhood is a hot country, amma lives there.
The sky has turned the colour of torn grass,

Think of the calf dragged away to Chenganacheri Fair,
Tiny tottering thing, snout wet with gooseberry juice.

You crouched in the dirt, staring and staring ,
Refused to come back in.

We had spiced pomfret, mangoes so ripe their sweat
Stained the damask tablecloth my dying mother left me.

Your grandfather's shadow hit the verandah.
He sat in his armchair, chewing on a cheroot.

Clouds swelled the mirror, broke its rosewood frame.
I saw your dead grandmother.

*Look to your child!* she cried.
I saw the mother cow, poor creature, her eye black,

Borderless, a lake you tried to drown in.
When ayah fished you out, your dress was soiled

With torn grass,
Your muslin petticoat so filthy, I could not bear to touch it!

Remember how we sat on the verandah,
You and I, under a tinderbox sky,

Sun poking holes in the palmyra leaves,
Just like the summer your grandfather died,

When girls with umbrellas whispering catechisms
Passed by on the street, their petticoats billowing mist.

You recited some lines –
*A child said what is grass ?*

A poem, wasn't it, about a child tearing up grass
With both her hands, fetching it to her mother?

## *Pale Blouses*

Rice blades in a muddy field,
Fretted gold bands fit for a dowry, tiny pearl-edged coffins.
So something else is wordless, as Chekov might have said.

Amma is fearful her babies will be girls,
But she wants them to be the sisters she never had,
Three girls skipping in the gravelled courtyard, tugging
    painted spools of thread.

Three sisters, as in the play she read, holding hands, longing
    to flee.
First sister melted her eyes into stones so no one could see,
Under her breath she sang songs of the monsoon wind.

Second sister trembled like a fox when its fur is stripped,
No one could bear the cadence of her cries.
Third sister took a strip of silk from grandmother's wedding
    sari,

Called out to the man in the crescent moon,
Sky Tailor come, it's time to set up your sewing machine on
    amma's verandah,
Time to snip the monsoon mist, stitch us pale blouses, help
    us make do.

## *South of the Nilgiris*

My son who is young
just six this year
knows the red soil of our land

Turning it in his palm
he said
'My sister is this earth
I am water
we will mix together.'

I heard this in a dream

He pointed at my belly
watermelon swollen
streaked as if mud

had dribbled over
lighter flesh

'I am glad
I was not born a girl.
I will never hold that weight
in my belly.'

He spun on his heels,
on his lean shoulders
I saw wings of bone
pale as the stones of Kozhencheri

'Mother!' he laughed
'You know I am not a girl!'

Under my ribs
she turned
his unborn sister,
green as a wave
on the southern coast
ready to overwhelm me,
overwhelm even the distant hills.

## *Gujarat Poems*

### *Amrita*

1
I was dressed
in a fine muslin
sari over which
I wore a fur coat.

Behind me an old
man with camera.
Picture perfect
nothing
cast a shadow.

2
My father
Umrao Singh
fasted for
fifteen days
took a photo
of himself
in skimpy
loin cloth.
Waist delicate
as a heron's neck.

Later my nephew

played with light,
set us edge
to edge.
In time's transparency
father and I
shone bright.

3

Nights I get no rest.
A rubber ball
bounces off
Parisian tapestries,
lands in my fur coat
splashes me.

Hold me
hold me a child cries.
My name is
Yunus.
Yunus can you hear me?

He stands there
half naked,
his green shirt
torn, flapping.
His belly and ribs
smoking.

He skips away.
I see his bottom
burst like a raw fruit
with the flames
they tossed him in

I put out my arms
to touch him
but father's
tripod
trips me up.

4
I want to whisper
I am Amrita
sweet
as burnt gold
in the dargah
of Wali Gujerati.

Here are my paints
my brushes
bright as bone.
Come to me.

## *Searching for a Tomb Over which They Paved a Road*

Where is the tomb
of Wali Gujerati?
Gold leaf scatters
in the wind.
His poems cry out for feet
hands, throat
for genitals and mouth.
Surat has forgotten him.
He sang her praises
to the moon.
And now?
*Where is my skin*
*my bones?*
*I am the poet of a city*
*in ruins*
*burnt by the sun*
*bound to the moon.*
The reeds
by the river
are lashed to swords
*My dust is in the mouth*
*of the bloodied rose.*

## *Letters to Gandhi*

### *Slow Dancing*

Dear Mr. Gandhi
please say something
about the carnage in your home state.

How did you feel when they shut
the gates of Sabermati Ashram
that February night

and the wounded clung outside?
What has happened to ahimsa?
Is it just for the birds and the bees?

What lips, what soles
swarmed across the river?
Is it hot on the other side?

O so many questions sir,
I cannot help myself
I cannot shut my mouth.

It's hard to hear you,
birds peck at  sounds
maggots gnaw since

even syllables have skin.
The kingdom of heaven
is tiny as a mustard seed

and you have crawled therein.
Mist pours from mango trees,
the moon soars in a sea of blood.

I see you at the rim of heaven
grown older still, bewildered, stooped
dhoti flecked with drops of mud,

face seared by a moon
that has nothing
except its own inhuman glow,

the archipelago of light
afloat in monsoon air
where souls frail as pinpricks go.

Dear Mr. Gandhi
please talk to me now.
I am slow dancing

in the the dark
with the untimely dead
and that is all I know.

## *Bengali Market*

Dear Mr. Gandhi
It was cold the day the masjid
was torn down stone by stone,
colder still at the heart of Delhi

Ten years later entering Bengali market
I saw a street filled with bicycles
girls with rushing hair, boys in bright caps
I heard a voice cry

*Can you describe this?*
It sounded like a voice
from a city crusted with snow
to the far north of the Asian continent.

I saw him then, your grandson
in a rusty three-wheeler
wrapped up in what wools he could muster.
Behind him in red letters

a sign: **Dr. Gandhi's Clinic.**
So he said, embracing me, you've come back.
Then pointing to the clinic —
It's not that I'm sick

that gentleman gets my mail and I his.
That is why I am perched in this contraption.

I cannot stay long, it is Id ul Fitr.
I must greet friends in Old Delhi, wish them well.

Later he sought me out in dreams.
In a high kitchen in sharp sunlight
dressed in a khadi kurta, baggy jeans.
He touched my throat in greeting.

Listen my sweet, for half of each year,
after the carriage was set on fire
after the Gujarat killings,
I disappear into darkness.

In our country there are two million dead
and more for whom no rites were said.
No land on earth can bear this.
Rivers are criss-crossed with blood.

All day I hear the scissor bird cry
*cut cut cut cut cut*
It is the bird Kalidasa heard
as he stood singing of buried love.

Now our boys and girls take
flight on rusty bicycles.
Will we be cured? I cried
And he: We have no tryst with destiny.

My hands like yours are stained
with the juice of the pomegranate.
Please don't ask for my address.
I am in and out of Bengali market.

## *Gandhi's Bicycle (My Muse Comes to Me)*

I come to you with a jute bag
filled with bits of cloth
marked with the colours of heaven.
I have meditated long and hard on the poems
you read at the Akademi.
In 'Ancestors' you have grandparents

male and female on wheels
cycling around ground zero.
Bipedality is no longer possible.

The earth is cut from underfoot
Have you seen the photo
of Gandhi on his bicycle, in South Africa?

He tried to walk the earth
the British made fun of him
also for the way he dressed.

Catastrophe drove you to
a grandmother in a sari on a bicycle
furiously pedalling where the towers

once stood, also a grandfather, I presume
with briefcase marked 'Lyric'.
But don't lose sight of Epic.

That very month, that very day,
September 11th in 1893,
Swami Vivekananda stood in Chicago

a dark rose on its stalk.
Chicago is in the midwest of course —
Sisters and brothers of America — he began

and there was thunderous applause.
How many would dare say that now.
But we need to say that you and I

even in the teeth of war. Come closer now.
do you hear the still sad music
of children killed in Godhra and Naroda Patiya

Come closer to this table, cut
from a tamarind tree in my grandfather's garden.
Each poet needs a table
to lay her wares out, don't you agree?
You can write your poems here
so they gather the sour sweet light of eternity.

One last thing, please don't
keep writing letters to Gandhiji.

He has gone through so much already.

Sometimes I dream he's hidden
in a cupboard with three doors
where he's also stashed his bicycle.

Notes to *'Letters to Gandhi'*

On September 11, 2002, I was in Ahmedabad to visit the relief camps for the survivors of ethnic violence. 'Letters to Gandhi' could not have come into being without two friends whose love reaches through the years: Svati Joshi who drew me back to Ahmedabad; Ramu Gandhi who always listened to me.

*Amrita:* Inspired by the digital photomontages of Vivan Sundaram's *Retake of Amrita.* I imagine Amrita Sher-Gil speaking after the Gujarat atrocities. The child Yunus I saw in a relief camp in Ahmedabad.

*Seaching for a Tomb:* During the carnage in Gujarat, the tomb of the seventeenth century Muslim poet, Wali Gujerati (also known as Wali Deccani) was torn down by Hindu extremists.

*Bengali Market:* The voice of Anna Akhmatova ('Instead of a Preface', *Requiem*) with a question someone asked her, echoed in my ear: 'Can you describe this?' In this poem I hear Akhmatova's voice, coming from the far north.

## SAMPURNA CHATTARJI

### *Mother and Daughter: A Duet*

When she gets angry she smiles
and sweetly excusing herself
she flees to the kitchen
and picks up the knife.
There, with a wild and murderous rage,
she chops and cuts and slices and dices
carrots potatoes cauliflower and cabbage:
the picture of a dutiful wife.
She weeps over onions
she gouges out eyes
she grinds her teeth with the spices
and she roasts and she fries.
She burns the milk she churns the curd
she minces the meat and she utters not a word.
She boils the water.
She simmers the tea.
She teaches her daughter:
"Girl, don't you be like me."
. . .
The last thing I want,
*mother,*
is to grow up
to be you.
So patient

so docile
so kind and so mild.
So eager to wait upon
your husband and child.
So loving
so slaving over a hot fire.
So quick
to whip up a meal or a snack.
So fleet with your fingers
with a stitch or a tack.
So silent in grief
so alone so bereaved
so forgotten
so left behind
so taken for granted and under-achieved.
So blamed
so worried
so self-defeated so harried
so sad
so glad
to be a mother and a wife all your life.

No,
I won't be you.
Never. Not me.
But first,
I'll just get my husband
his tea.

## *Fairytale*

Rubies, spill your blood on my throat.
Emeralds, your envy.
Beauty, leave some rags for me
that I might presume to be
a woman: beautiful bedecked believable.

Mutilated, yes,
pierced at the navel and the groin,
lips puckered in disdain.
A steep price but what the hell.
I'm tired of being such a beast,

long-toothed and four-eyed.
Despised and denied
the peculiar joys
of being whistled at and wolfed down
by male eyes.

Let me pretend, then.
Slashed and bound and painted
in some arabesque of lip and lash,
mark on head, mole on chin,
so frightened so frightening.

And when I'm done, let me take
this mirror and break
seven years of bad luck

into your kind, observant,
fairy godmother face.

## *Object Lesson: Three*

*Find yourself a cup of tea; the teapot is behind you. Now tell me about hundreds of things.*

– Saki

Imbibe in little sips the story
through your lips.
Savour the scandal.
Notice the line of her kimono sleeves
parting the way as she leaves.
Mark the angle of his body
as he shows her out (lets her in).
Mark the compliance of her maid's
helpful pout her little grin.
And if you have the time, as you should,
notice the niceties of the hairdos
the mistress elegantly coiffured
against stress the maid's casual strands
coming loose.

Hierarchies painted in place
as you hold the cup to your face
and turn it around for what may be
another side to this story.

Where

a cunning courtier and a Machiavellian monk prepare to
show in (let out)
two noblewomen poised between indecision and doubt.

A cold day.
Put the lid on it.
Keep the stories warm.

## *Object Lesson: Seven*

*Chopsticks are to the fingers what stilts are to the legs.*
– Tong Sing,
*The Chinese Book of Wisdom*

Bug-eyed blue fish
swim smoothly on porcelain.
Fingers twirl
fin chasing tail in a flail
of multiplying moves.
The frozen panic
of being needed
no longer.

One stick chopped into two.
Its perfect partner lies useless
next to the bowl pierced
by an identical hole

eye of the needle letting in
a single thread of light.

No future here
carrying delicate morsels
to celibate mouths.
Easy now.
What's broken
needs handling with care.

## *Where Do I Put This Love*

Where do I put this love, this open need for gentleness?
Put it in a closed place.
Some place small,
like a little tin box, the kind you hid under the bed,
a tight, closed, small and secret space
hidden in a darkness bigger, darker, safer.
Some place closed and small,
like a fist, holding nothing more momentous
than a curl perhaps, a coin, a piece of chocolate quickly
melting, a vein, the place where lines cross,
put there by someone bigger, wiser, safer.
Some place warm and closed and small
like the O of your mouth, closing around a sticky red sweet,
a word you have just learnt, a breath
you have just taken and are holding, small and sweet,
for the time when you might feel bigger, stronger, safer.

Or, put it out in the open.
By a window, perhaps, with branches in it,
and two nests, crows, a couple minding their own business,
their eggs waiting to hatch
into the open.
Or in the living room, on the centre table,
next to the large glass bowl of cut flowers,
attracting no attention, invisible
next to that headiness, that smell
of wanting to be elsewhere in those flagrant petals,
back where they belong, somewhere out in the open.
The wide-open open, a field, a paddy field,
green from eye to sky, the sky a circle
around your thrown-back head, trying to see
behind beyond the circumference of the earth,
the way the horizon curves and curves, closed and
    continuous
circling endlessly into the open.

Open or closed, it flutters,
heart, wing, eyelash, pulse, beat, tremor,
turning,
turning slowly inwards, outwards, onwards,
looking for sun, shade, sorrow, looking
for a place it might finally rest, contained
and uncontainable.

## *Let No One*

It was in a Russian fairytale that I saw him first, the brave
boy with the heart in his hand.
It didn't seem strange, a lantern made of vein and cavity, left
ventricle and right valve.
I didn't wonder how the boy breathed as he walked, didn't
wonder what pumped the

muscles in his legs, didn't marvel at how a body could
survive, heartless, and strong.
I did wonder at the light that came from his heart, the strong
blue-white light that
threw a path straight and simple through the trees. Perhaps it
was yellow, it's been

so long I can hardly tell what's right, and what's left of
memory. Perhaps it was
his face that was blue with breathing. I have known what it is
like to be blue with breathing, in a fairytale all my own. I
have known, in the way children know things

that I too was once that blue-lipped boy. Only I didn't have
to be brave, someone else was brave for me. *I was the*
*heart he held in his hand, close to his hollow thumping chest.*
*He ran with me – his heart – in his hand, in the light that*
*came from the trees. It was*

*night and there were stones that he might have stumbled over.*

But it's the boy I'm thinking about now. I wish I
remembered his name. The clarion call of his name on
my lips. Or even the name of the forest. Was it the Black
Forest? The peril he was

fleeing from, the people he was saving, seeing what must be
done in the split-second before he tore out his heart.
How it must have bled. How it must have shocked the
people that he led, not large, but little, a little boy with a
large heart, bleeding his way towards

safety, towards the edge that is the end of terror and the
beginning of sleep. As they stumbled, safe, into the day,
did anyone turn to the boy? The story didn't say. Sure he
was a hero, and they gave him a Name. But did he die?
Did he find a lap to lie in as he

died? Did someone smooth the sweating hair off his brow?
Where is his mother now? Of course he died. Hollow
chest raw with an open wound, he died, his heart in his
hand.
In the unforgiving light of day the heart looked grey and
lifeless, a mass of useless tissue,

a lump of lard, a hard ungiving knot of bone. And in that
blue-white light of very-early- morning in a Russian
fairytale, even the yellow-flame sun could not pierce
through with what he really needed, then. The kiss of
warmth on his cheek, the reversal that other tales

have told so well, blood flooding into stone, tissues healing,
feeling their way into the knittedness of flesh, the spell of
magic ointments, the smell of smoking herbs. Someone
should have moved a mountain for him then, someone
should have walked in the guise of

a mighty lion. He was, after all, very small. He needed
saving too. *Let no one put one step on the ground, the second
on his palm, the third on his head. Let no one enter the forest
riddled with by-ways and hope to see light, again.* And if
they do, let no one speak

of flight again,
let no one speak
of love.

## RUKMINI BHAYA NAIR

### *Reasons*

Some write to remember, others
To forget
                    But when the vagrant
Winds of autumn sweep
Into a woman's mind
She writes
                    To surrender, she wants
To be met . . .

Loneliness
                    Like dry strokes fading
In the inkwells of her heart
                    A woman
Writes her epitaph
                    With slow regret
While summer's green lustre fades
Into death unto death . . .

Words delight her
For just one prancing spring
                    They flash
And burn and dance!—an endless
Unthinking
                    Mating is so simple then
That no woman dreams

Of fate . . .

The white flowers of winter
Open very late
                    Under moist earth they
Wait and they wait
For meanings to root and syllables
Resonate
And in the end a woman writes as
Nature dictates . . .

## *Flame*

Prometheus, you towering fool,
You blithering ass, you nincompoop.

Far from being a wily Greek, you're
Indian, judging by your behaviour.

Pyromania has always been something
Of a subcontinental speciality.

Producers of match-stick limbs, match-box
Torsos, holding zillion conflagrations

We burn brides, and we burn widows.
Immolation's the rage even with kiddos.

Circa 1990. From our beloved Ram, in
Antiquity, trace an unbroken line.

Here's a charming festival of lights

Extinguishing that old devil, Ravana

And here at Sriperumbudur, Ramanuja's
Birthplace, town where temples glow,

An inheritor, political prince, blown
To bits by Lankan furies, now known

Through little but his Lotto shoes.
Irony at the short end of a fuse.

We always took fire dead seriously,
Using it to test involvement, chastity,

And other such doubtful propositions,
Love and worship qualified our position.

You were like us in this, loving fire.
But to play with it, rub flints to see

Sparks fly for the fun of it, was folly.
To treat Agni as a household appliance,

Cooker, night lantern, warm blanket, all
Rolled into one, the height of arrogance!

He a male God, you only a friendly giant.
Prometheus, it takes a woman to be defiant.

## *Gulmohur*
*(Freedom Song in a Minor Key)*

On a windy day like this
The rain clouds descend
Rough, tough, male

And the gulmohur
Forgets she is a tree
Rooted to the ground

Everything else thrusts
Upwards, red gold kites
Terriers' pricking ears

Alert to a drum of thunder
Eagles, and stiffish buds
On small, petulant plants

These rise to teasing bait
The short glamour of sex
Then why not the gulmohur?

*Why not she?*

Today, the sky is a bowl
Each ribbed gulmohur leaf
An imprisoned angel-fish

Swimming round and round
In the cold, grey lucency
Of the hooligan monsoons

But unable to escape, play
Her deft wit off against
A loutish rain-cloud

The gulmohur loses heart
Sheds her vivacious fins
Her wild, scarlet flowers

Is this the nature of a tree
To be tied down eternally
Or can the gulmohur be free

*Can she?*

## *Hermaphrodite Longings*

Only Sappho prepared me

Only Sappho of Lesbos, her nipples dry and her
Words flowing on the wrinkled parchment
Like milk

Only Sappho wrote, at the end of her womanhood
Wise with the love of both her sexes
Dying in Eressos under tyrants
Under the potent stars . . .

*Even in Hades I am with you*
*Andromeda . . . Gongyla . . . My desire feeds*
*On your beauty, Gongyla. Each time I see your gown*

*I am made weak and happy . . . You of all women whom*
*I most desire, come to me again . . .*

Sappho, queen of subtexts, knowing
She would be burnt in a thousand years
By Gregory of Rome . . . That she would turn
Like an old crone's memory into a flickering
Heap of papyrus cinders, ignited by some silly man

Only Sappho imagined history as a woman's body . . .
And who but a woman could own a woman's body?

Sappho's logic was as flawless as her verse. History
Did not belong to the bawdy boys . . . It did not
Rest with the emperor hacks who thought they had it
Taped. History was a rage of longing, a storm of enduring
And history got its own back on the men who mounted it . . .

History takes the shape of a woman and it is a woman
Knows best the rounded feel of a woman's buttocks
How to rub with scented violet, cassia and myrrh
The tender insides of those angular elbows . . . sharp,
delicious
Tickle of her nails, her Medusa smile . . . these are women's
skills . . .

True histories are histories of women in love.

Catullus drinking to Lesbia had to have Sappho
As his model. There was no way out. It was
Just the way history staked out a man.
Got him. Six hundred years before Catullus
Used her, Sappho meditated on this secret . . .

A man in love must become a woman
Before he is done with loving
And every poet, Catullus included
Enters history through the body of a woman
In this rich canal of birth, his nemesis, his aches . . .

Sappho knew well

That scored, transvestite passage
That politic mixing
Of the sexes

Then listen, Sappho, to this . . .

A man snatched at me this afternoon
He was a woman, his eyes rimmed with
Kohl, the veins red with memory. I could not
Look at him. My eyes fell . . .

Because it was your face

It was your face I saw
In the mutilated body, in the coarse

Horsewhip tactics of that *hijra*, scintillating with oils
Jasmine, the blouse a gaudy trap, her hand
Across me, a sinewy band of teak . . . I could not
Pass . . . I had to face

Your terrible longing, Sappho

The centuries have changed. In these three thousand years
Even Andromeda, lying so still in her starry bed
Has altered her position a little, but this has not
Changed . . . Every man has memories of being a woman
And women know that they have been gods
At one time or another . . . *Ardhanarishwara*
Half-woman god . . . You knew him . . .

Sappho in Indica, crossing boundaries

You *were* him . . . *Ardhanarishwara*, enticingly chaste
Lover of lovers, you were that divided god . . .
Peerless hermaphrodite, soft as woman's silk
Rough as the knuckles of a man . . . And you are

This lewd woman who bars my way . . .

You snatched my purse this afternoon
Admit it. You robbed me of my possessions
For which favours I owe you, Sappho . . .

Because you showed me how love strips down
How it is the territory of eunuchs and gays
Of the women of Lesbos, transvestites
Slaves, hermaphrodites, the poxy
Apple-cheeked seventeenth century brats
Playing Artemis and Diana, of the specialist
Men of Indica, sinuous *narivesham* dancers
Performing only as women, of housewives
Bar-girls, of every damned woman . . .

And only then of the straight men
The fathers and the patrons, the heterosexual
Saints . . . These stand outside the gates of love

Only you, Sappho, might have warned the ladies of Eressos

Love is a marauder, attacking from the margins
It has no great estates, powers, privileges
Alley cat of history in a diamond collar, love
Survives by stealth, snatching at beauty . . .

Summon, Sappho, your alabaster memories of Atthis

*You lay in wait behind a laurel tree . . . You*
*A woman wanderer like me . . . I barely*
*Heard you, my darling . . . You came*
*In your trim garments . . . And suddenly*
*Beauty of your garments!*

That was love at work. It jumped the petty fences . . .
Crossed the sea of Indica and Attica, it was
History swishing into the dream world of Hades . . .

Sappho, this was the catastrophe you feared

*Hermes came to me in a dream. I said*
*My master, I am altogether lost . . .*
*And my many riches do not console me*
*I care only . . . to die . . . and to watch the dewy lotus*
*Along the banks of Acheron, river of hell . . .*

Only you, Sappho, mourned so completely
When love died at the bejewelled pontiff's hands . . .
You alone took Kleis, your beloved daughter
In your austere arms and did not flinch as you told her . . .

*I have no embroidered head-band for you, Kleis*
*And no idea where to find one*
*While Myrsilos rules in Mytilene . . . The bright*
*Ribbon reminds me of those days when our*
*Enemies were in exile . . . O Kleis . . .*

Sappho, history comes winding back
Persistent as a woman . . .

How you shocked me, Sappho!
But I see now why you wore
The face of a eunuch this afternoon, held me

Captive with your street-smart tongue, straining
Under a shameless lift of skirts, that sequinned
Body, to reveal your damaged sex . . .

You crossed black Acheron, Sappho, to rob me of my vanity

Kleis in Indica, distracted by bright ribbons
Sappho does not spare her daughters wherever they   are . . .

In Indica, in Hades

Sappho, *Ardhanarishwara*
Sings to her vulnerable daughters
In the perfect, androgynous voice of God . . .

Only Sappho shows

The true hermaphrodite face of love
Under the still moon, the harsh
Bullying stars . . .

## *Margins, Ma(i)nstream*

A woman is a thing apart.
She is bracketed off, a
Comma, semicolon, at most
A lower case letter, lost

In the literate circus.
She is just a striptease
Artist, but when she speaks
Her poems bite, ferocious.

Rhyme and shape, primitive
Beasts, come tamed to her
Endangered species, they
Recognize her desperation.

She wants, she badly wants
Not a fresh lover, strongman
Or clown, but a new language
In which to hold her own.

## TEMSULA AO

### *Trophies**

It is one of those crazy nights yet again;
the air is rent by blood-curdling yells
of the warriors come home
with enemy heads which will hang
from the skull-tree in the village field

The heads will sway gently
with unseeing eyes and hair
matted by their own blood,
and standing below them
the warriors will hurl insults
at the gory trophies and caper wildly
shrieking with the madness of new wine

But the merry-making will only worsen
the fatigue of warfare, overcoming
the weary, blood-caked warriors;
they will soon shuffle about, too weary
to sing and dance and will collapse
in ungainly heaps from the drunken stupor,
and at first cock-crow
will stumble unsteadily home.

These men, the father
of my child among them,

are an absurd lot,
rejoicing over some ugly
severed heads, foolishly unmindful
about marauding animals
devastating standing crops
and threatening women and children.

All they seem to ever care for
is the glory in bringing home
an enemy head to prove
that they are heroes
while the home-fires go unlit.

I've witnessed this sorry spectacle
countless times and shared the misery
with other women whose husbands too
indulge in such meaningless heroics.

I do not know what
the other women think
but I can no longer
remain silent about
this senseless pursuit
after vain glory
and vacuous reward.

This dawn when he staggers in
I shall ignore him and
pinch my sleeping child

to make him cry
and when he asks me why

I shall confront him and say,
'You may rejoice over your bloody trophies
but enemy heads will never fill
my child's empty belly,
nor quench my need for a body
untainted by another's blood
to douse the heat of summer
and ignite the cold of winter

and if you do not heed me
I may soon return to my parents
a widow and your son
the orphan of a reckless father'

* Refers to the Naga custom of chopping off the heads of slain enemies in warfare and bringing them home as trophies, for public display at a central place. Head-takers were considered to be heroes and such warriors earned the right to wear special ornaments and give Feasts of Merit to the entire village as a mark of their elevated status in society.

## *The Leaf-Shredder**

There is a bent old woman sitting
On a rickety bamboo platform, shooing
The village chicks away from the paddy
Spread out to dry in the winter sun

She once held court in this little cottage
Beyond the village gate
Where fierce-looking warriors received
Fear-killing potions before a dreaded fight.

It was to her door women of all ages
Came with their unspeakable pains
Spilling their grief to the ageless priestess
With eager hopes for just redress.

But time has finally intervened
To dispel the ambience of that life
Through natural infirmity
And trivial domesticity.

The all-seeing glint has left her eyes
And lethargy stalks her tired limbs
While the revelations of the shredded leaves
Become a web of hazy memories.

Sometimes her frazzled mind sifts
From its distant past a dream-like montage

Of a frantic wife who came to her one day
Driven wild by her husband's threat

'Grandmother, please help me,
My man means to turn me away
And take another wife
If I don't give him a son.'

She saw the fear in the young eyes
And asked her gently 'Why, my child
Aren't you his wife?
Don't you let him touch you?'

'Yes, grandmother, I have been wife to him
For three years now and he puts
His seed in me day and night
But the monthly flood sweeps it away.

He calls me barren and says I am a curse
On his clan and demands a son by next harvest
Or he'll take another woman who will
Hold his seed and give him sons.'

The old woman still remembers
How the frightened eyes concentrated
On the leaf she shredded to determine
The mystery of the young wife's despair.

When she finished divining
She looked at the hopeful wife
And whispered 'Go home my child,
You will bear many sons'

She chuckles now in recalling
The part she left unsaid, and how
The woman bore many sons
But for another man.

She remembers at times the vast forests
Where she roamed freely
Venturing into the darkest depths
Where even the bravest did not dare

It was a home away from home
Where she conversed with
The spirits of the earth
To ferret the secrets of their hearts.

She talked to all the creatures,
Sometimes pilfering gifts
From their nests and burrows
To augment her magic hoard.

She scoured the deepest forests
In search of the rare mushrooms
Ghoulish brown and malodorous
Vital for concocting potent potions

To invigorate petrified warriors
Before dreaded battles so that
They could disdain their fears
And die dreaming of promised glory.

She remembers once chancing upon an ant
Enacting a strange dance with her spindly legs
In frantic communication with a smug beetle
Crying out in frightened squeaks,

'Brother, mother earth's heart is trembling
The beasts are crazed with panic and
There is an acrid smell in the air
Some great calamity will surely befall us.'

The beetle dismissed her saying
How could she, a pitiable creature,
Assume to foretell what only
Diviners and leaf-shredders knew?

As she thinks of this, the old seer shudders
Recalling the horrors of the killer-quake
And marvels at the uncanny accuracy
Of the tiny creature's instinctive prophecy.

For the old woman on the rickety platform
These are ephemeral vignettes from a trance-like life,
Impinging on her present situation,
So disengaged from her distant past.

Only the matted hair and raggedy clothes,
Still smelling of forests and their secrets
Darkly hint at a surreal history, beyond
The range of human calculation

As she sits patiently on the rickety platform
Waiting to pass on to the great unknown
A persistent dream-like question
Impedes the pace of transition

Wondering if anyone had ever
Read her forlorn destiny
In the shreds
Of a ravished virgin leaf.

* According to the oral tradition of the Aos, there were some special men and women who were endowed with powers to read the future. They were called *Arasentsur*, and the most common practice among them was to shred the leaf called 'aam' in order to predict futures and also to prescribe appropriate rituals as curatives for different diseases.

### *Why Not / Woman to Man*

When you say I am not
The prettiest or the fairest

I am not angry
As I know I am no great beauty

I've also heard that you once
Snubbed a maiden, pretty but lazy

Saying, 'My sons' eyes
Will not fill their bellies.'

My skin, you say is dark
What of it, if I've caught your mark?

As for you, when you laugh
I see a broken tooth

What did you do?
Bite off a tiger's tooth?

You want me to wait
Till harvest time to build a house

But I must tell you this.

The maternal uncle from the Onger's* house
Came to father saying

A house was waiting
All made of timber and tin

I said, why do I need a house like that
When I've always lived with bamboo and thatch?

Mother protested, he is a good orator,
I asked her if his sleek tongue

Could set the traps to catch
Wild meat for my kitchen

He is handsome, mother persisted
But his dao* is blunt, I replied

Can such a tool clear
A jungle patch every year?

Mother was annoyed and predicted
I would end up an old maid.

She points out your faults
And calls me a fool but I tell her

You may be slow to speech
But your traps, I know, always spring.

Your face is like a craggy mountain

But the dao in your belt outshines the sun

And when the men play tug-of-war
I always see you at the anchor

With steady pace other men walk to fields
But with you I see only running feet

In your Arju* too I hear
You are the best storyteller

And also that you have beaten
Every other wrestler of your age-set.

So when your maternal uncle comes
I shall tell my mother to tell my father

That his daughter prefers
The house of bamboo and thatch

Where the bonfire of our hearts
Will shame the flames of the hearth

And in that house I shall place
My precious loom

To weave you a langtem*every season
And a sunak* at every Moatsu*

* *Onger:* Headman of the village.

* *Dao:* A cutting implement used by men to cut trees and shrubs.

* *Arju:* Young men's dormitory among the Aos.

* *Langtem:* Loincloth for covering male genitals.

* *Sunak:* A traditional Ao-Naga shawl for men made of faded indigo and black yarn.

* *Moatsu:* Spring festival of the Aos, celebrated after sowing, to invoke God's blessings for a plentiful harvest.

## *Why Not / Man to Woman*

Woman, let me tell you the reasons
Why I have courted you these many seasons.

You may not be the prettiest
Nor the fairest of the village maidens

But when you smile
I see my world lit up in your face

The rhododendron you wear in your ear
Glows like the flame in my heart

The curves on your calves
Shimmer like ripe bananas

And golden guavas
Pale before your maiden buds.

When you walk, your swaying hips
Ripple with life's new promise

And when you dance on festive days
The earth rings out with your beads and bells

At harvest when you gather the sheaves
The autumn sunshine gilds your limbs

When you sit at the loom
You seem to weave my dream

Like the sunak you gave me
This last Moatsu day

And every time I wear this dream-cloth
I dare think you will not say no.

Woman, what more can I say
To convince you why

I want you by my fireside
To assuage my other fire?

After the harvest is over
I shall build a new house*

It will only be of thatch and bamboo
But built with love for you

When the time is right
My maternal uncle will bring my offer in the night

So tell your mother to tell your father
To accept my offer

For I am an honest hard-working farmer
Who will always cherish his daughter

Oh woman, what more can I do
To convince you

That I want you with a yearning
Stronger than the jhum* burning?

And as I dream and wait
Turn away the others from your hut.

But when I come, open the door wide
And let me walk to next year's jhum by your side.

* Before an Ao man marries, he has to build a new house where he takes his wife to begin a new family.

* *Jhum:* a patch of land from where all vegetation is cleared and burnt to prepare it for cultivation.

## *Nowhere Boatman*

*According to traditional Ao-Naga belief, the souls of dead people have to pay some coins to the boatman on the river between the Land of the Living and the Land of the Dead to ferry them across to the other side, where, it is believed, they begin another existence.*

The riders on my boat often ask me
How long I have plied this trade
On the river between
The land of the living
And the land of the dead.

They even ask me
How old I am,
As if knowing my age
Has anything to do with their being
On my boat for their last ride
From the land of the living.

But on some slack days I feel like
Telling them to go ask
The sky who sees it all
Or the wind who hears it all
And even the river itself
Who has borne countless others
Like them across.

If some persist on prying
I shall send the pesky souls

To the tree-stump whose belly
Is now my boat, to tell them
How old is old?

Anyway, what has age to do with dying
And of what use this irrelevant knowledge
When they are already pledged
On a one-way journey
To their destiny?

But of late I've become
Deeply disturbed
To realize that no one
Has ever enquired
Who I am and of which clan
And most important of all
Where I belong:
The land they have left
Or the one they are going to?

A soul without a status,
Is how I see myself
Fated to ply my trade
On this designated route.

On such depressing days I jingle
The miserable pile of small coins
That litters the pit of my boat
And ask myself

What advantage
This petty exchange
For the unremitting service
Of re-locating well-defined souls
In preordained spaces?

When my own immaterial
Existence knows not
Whether it can claim
Any kinship with the living
Or one day join the dead
On a final crossing.

Yet I continue to exist,
An ageless, nameless
Indispensable anomaly,
The nowhere boatman
On the river between
Two irreconcilable worlds.

## MENKA SHIVDASANI

### *Spring-Cleaning*

That was your skull on the bottom shelf,
staring socketless at my ankle.
It was a surprise find among those
bunches of old clothes.
Once I would have screamed;
now I've learned to discard
what doesn't fit, and especially, all that's ugly.

Carelessly draped on a hanger, I found an arm
leaning bonily towards the perfumes;
in another corner, a dislocated knee.
Did you run away so fast, you broke your leg?
I wish you'd wipe that foolish
toothless grin off your stupid face.
You needn't be embarrassed about
letting me down. Other men have too, and they
didn't disintegrate like you.

What the hell
does one do with human remains?
Should I put them in the waste basket,
let the sweeper see? Or, struggling under the weight,
dump a gunny bag off the beach?

You really are a nuisance, turning up

on a lethargic Sunday. Now go away.
When I want to say hello, I'd rather
walk up to the graveyard
with a sweet-smelling bunch of flowers,
look sad, and pretend
you are still below the earth.

## *Why Rabbits Never Sleep*

Lettuce is Nature's sedative, I read somewhere,
so at three a.m., I finally
decided to make a little salad.
There were cockroaches in the refrigerator
but I washed the vegetable well, then peeled
layer after layer, startling a sleepy worm
that had crawled indignantly from beneath the leaves.
But the pieces lay untidily, splashed across the plate,
like splotches of sun on the street;
so I tried another strategy—common, really,
any housewife-poet will know it.

I took a knife, its blade seductive in the dark,
and I chopped. The fragments, I noticed, as I yawned,
had begun to take the most extraordinary shapes.
Somewhere I recognised a bride,
her toenails turned to ash,
a mother-in-law and husband shut the door.
Another piece bore the face of a wicked politician;
a third was a child with eyes wide open.

And why did the dish resemble
a wounded Hiroshima?

I went at it like the smiling Nazi
in a half-remembered film, who invited
his prisoner to lunch, then demonstrated
the art of cutting carrots.
'Chop, chop,' he said, and as the slices fell,
still smiling, hacked the prisoner's finger off,
two actually, with the words, 'Chop, chop,'
and another smile.

That night, I discovered the reason
rabbits never seem to sleep.

## *The Quality of Darkness*

When the quality of darkness is a stain
and a pound of flesh is simply not enough,
you set your sights on what else you can maim
and hope that history will one day call your bluff.

You hold the paper knife in your hand.
It is not sharp enough to cut or brand.
This quality of darkness seeps across the land

and brothers become shadows,
sister turns to stone.

You trip upon a boundary wall,
gnaw upon a bone.

An unhinged brick leaves a stain upon your hand.
You try to get up, find you cannot stand
while darkness seeps across the land

and mother turns to maniac,
father turns to ash.
You wipe the stain of a brick away,
find it has left a gash

but in the heat of this quiet night
you hover, blot-like, find you cannot fight

and as the gash turns dry upon your palm,
you pick the brick off unhinged walls, let fly.
One of you tonight is going to die

and who will know as the darkness swoops on you?

## *Epitaph*

The thing to do
is feel the texture of the page
still white before the lines form,
touch the smoothness of its skin,
refined unlike the bark
once peeled away.

The trouble is,
we do not wear white
on the wedding day.
My religion calls for blood,
redness draped across the eyes,
wrapped tight around the skin.
But lines form anyway,
alphabets rounded like shoulders
or flat as hair upon the arm.
The story begins like a wrinkle on the face
and does not end
when the wrinkles freeze.

But that is when the surface
turns to white and I hold my pain
in its plastic tube
let the fluid fall.

That's when the poem writes itself
like an epitaph.

## *Kitchen Dreams*

Sniffing through the spices, nuzzling your way through,
twisting between tables, is that really you?
Whistling past the cookers, winking from the floor,
are you that whimsical friend  she used to know before

she got into this grinder with chili, onion, lime,
chopped up among the veggies, content but marking time?
Is that really you calling from the door?
She's lost her way to freedom, doesn't know it any more

because she's in this mess of nappy rash and goo,
alone except for the wailing of a baby not yet two.
She ties herself in knots as she twists her graying hair;
does she  know her way to freedom, would she really dare

to find herself past the crossroads of childhood left behind,
beyond that dusty hallway where once she had a mind?
Sniffing through the spices, she faintly hears you call;
perhaps she'll join you soon; right now, she's played against
the wall

and the cooker's whistling freedoms; the fruit tray's full of
seed.
How does she deal with the knife-edge that slices every
need?
Tell her, friend, is that really you?

You used to speak of poetry, she thought your words were
true.
But now her life is whitewashed, the door is firmly shut.
She wants to shatter this security, instead she takes the blade
to cut
a portion of that lively brain that once she so well knew.
That may not be so good for her, but it will add flavour to
the stew

and she wouldn't change that for anything else; could you?

## *Marionette*

Go on,
tell your story.
The right things
must come right
to you; the world's
a wooden stage,
a box with nails,
go on.
Let them pull
the strings tonight,
you cannot put up
a fight, a little
wooden doll,
you little
fool.

Go on,
keep the show alive,
they're watching
from the floor,
waiting
to hear the story
that you've
been taught before.
Let someone
mouth the phrases
as you make
all the right faces,
wooden marionette,
the game's not
over yet.

Don't pull that
string so hard!
Don't break
this wooden heart,
see the mouth
will fall apart,
and if you don't
take care,
there'll be mayhem
at the fair,
or so you'd like to think
as though the world
is going to share

the wooden pain
of a wooden painted doll.

So go on,
tell your story,
don't collapse,
don't lose the thread.
You've only got
midway, it's a long way
to your bed.
The iron
is digging in,
but don't worry,
there's no soul,
just an empty space
for the nail
to fill the empty hole.

Come. Come,
come one, come all,
the show's about to start.
It's time to hear
the marionette,
watch her play
her part.
Don't worry about
the cost, this one
comes really cheap —
now behave yourself —

there she goes again! —
crumbling in a heap.

Now what on earth
are we going to do?

## MAMANG DAI

### *The Sorrow of Women*

They are talking about hunger.
They are saying there is an unquenchable fire
burning in our hearts.
My love, what shall I do?
I am thinking how I may lose you
to war, and big issues
more important than me.

Life is so hard, like this,
nobody knows why.
It is like fire.
It is like rainwater, sand, glass.
What shall I do, my love,
if my reflection disappears?

They are talking about a place
where rice flows on the streets
about where there is gold
in the leaves of trees,
they are talking about displacement
when the opium poppy was growing
dizzy in the sun,
happy, in a state of believing

And they are talking about escape,

about liberty, men and guns,
Ah, the urgency for survival!
But what will they do
not knowing the sorrow of women?

## *The Voice of the Mountain*

From where I sit on the high platform
I can see the ferry lights crossing
criss-crossing the big river

I know the town, the estuary mouth.
There beyond, the last bank
where the colour drains from heaven
I can outline the chapters of the world.

The other day a young man arrived from the village.
Because he could not speak
he brought a gift of fish
from the land of rivers.
It seems such acts are repeated:
We live in territories forever ancient and new,
and as we speak in changing languages
I, also, leave my spear leaning by the tree
and try to make a sign.

I am an old man sipping the breeze
that is forever young.
In my life I have lived many lives.

My voice is sea waves and mountain peaks,
in the transfer of symbols
I am the chance syllable that orders the world
instructed with history and miracles.

I am the desert and the rain.
The wild bird that sits in the west.
The past that recreates itself
and particles of life that clutch and cling
For thousands of years
I know, I know these things
as rocks know, burning in the sun's embrace,
about clouds, and sudden rain;
as I know a cloud is a cloud,
a cloud is this uncertain pulse
that sits over my heart.

In the end the universe yields nothing
except a dream of permanence.
Peace is a falsity.
A moment of rest comes after long combat:

From the east the warrior returns
with the blood of peonies.
I am the child who died at the edge of the world,
the distance between end and hope.
The star diagram that fell from the sky,
the summer that makes men weep.
I am the woman lost in translation

who survives with happiness to carry on.

I am the breath that opens the mouth of the canyon,
the sunlight on the tips of trees;
there, where the narrow gorge hastens the wind
I am the place where memory escapes
the myth of time,
I am the sleep in the mind of the mountain.

## *Incalculable Days*

What if I lose you to the crowd
By theft of reason
To the streets of summer
The petals of flowers,
Even to the chanting of prayers,
Coins, gold leaf . . .

What if—
At night the fan turns with the sound of engines
The distance hanging between us.
Happiness, unhappiness,
It does not matter.
No, not now,
In the incalculable days
Caught between the green bowl of earth
And life of glass
Together the scales of the dragon

And the roofs of houses
Are snared in the circle of heaven

There are many means of survival.
I see it in the streets every day.
In the courtyard of symbols
Someone like myself is crying
For the man who loved me.
Is it true
In the eyes of a thousand deities
I am mingled with chance and fate?

The sun burns.
The wind strokes every strand of my hair.
Amid the hordes of people,
The fleeting faces of strangers,
Incalculable as the days
Of stillness and motion
I am lost to the anguish of trees,
The sky and lakes, apparently asleep.

But I did not tell you
That I did not die.

# TAMIL

# KUTTI REVATHI

## *Not for sale*

Unable to dissolve the poverty line ever
I decided to sell my breasts.
Upon losing all other organs in an auction
I went to shop after shop . . .
Could not place them for sale amidst
Jewellery or fruit
Could not hang them on walls
Or on racks   like lingerie
In the toy shop for children
Children wanted nothing but these;
He returned them, saying the sale of toys had decreased
Adding that anyone would willingly keep them for rent

Now they are on rent
In schools
to nurse children.

*Translated by V. Padma*

## *Agony*

It was a mishap at the end of the rainy season.

The body of a huge tree fell down
Into the rain's lap;
Its roots were blinded by light
They died of fright.

Two people came silently
And started cutting the tree.
One
Thought of his father
On his death-bed;
The other,
Ashamed, recalled his wife's face
Twisted with tears after having sex.

The tree broke into two
Spreading the cries of birds over a corpse.

*Translated by V. Padma*

## SALMA

### *Midnight*

After my deliveries
At night
You search with dissatisfaction
For the innocence of my beauty
In familiar nudity.

Bloated body
And stretch-marked stomach
Disgust you,
You say.

Today or tomorrow
My body will never change,
I murmur
My voice lies buried
In the valley of silence.

True.
Yours isn't like mine
In declaration.
Out in the open.

Earlier
Your children might have been born
Somewhere for someone.

You can pride yourself
On not bearing any traces.

What can I do?
These stretch marks
Reveal my damage.
Not easy to repair.
This body is not paper to cut and paste.

Nature has been my worst betrayer
Worse than you.
Doesn't the first phase of my failure
Begin with you?

The second watch of the night
Overflows with dreams
More dangerous than the first.

In the first watch,
The tiger sits in the painting hung on the wall.
In this second watch of the night
It sits near my head
Staring at me intently.

*Translated by V. Padma*

## *My Ancestral House - I*

They set aside a time for it
well in advance

Then
from a body shrivelled
to a dry, wrinkled raisin,
a doctor
intense, yet detached
separates and plucks out
her uterus

There it lies
in the silent calm
of a water-filled vessel
A piece of raw meat
it floats
mysterious in its gleaming

I stare at that piece of flesh
which once held my life
a huge ache spears my heart
and arcs towards it
I mourn, later, I sorrow

So what if it has borne life
these many times
spawned in the toilet

a searing flame
a curse
her uterus

Perhaps
it is time now
time for its soul,
wrung dry,
after endless hunts
to seek repose.

A few minutes
before the appointed hour
she looks intently
at the light that lies
shattered outside her door
below the lattice-work
and says
in a voice drained of fear:

'From now on,
I'm a half-woman.'
These words hold
inside them
the burning violent anger of
loss
that takes from me forever
my heart's peace.

*Translated by V. Geetha*

## *Space*

I know
The sorrows of the broken chair
The curtain-less windows
The cobwebs on the clock
The midnight cockroaches that multiply
The loss of privacy in a latch-less bathroom.

I know
That all these jobs have to be completed
before the children return home.

Still, to this day,
I don't get one thing:
The attachment to this space as mine and
My exile from the ancient caves.

*Translated by V. Geetha*

## SUGANTHI SUBRAMANIAN

### *Untitled*

When my tins were filled with
Rice, dal, chilli and tamarind
And I had the T.V.
Newspapers and weeklies.
The woman opposite my house
Introduced herself in a language unknown to me
When she came to borrow green chillies.
My neighbour became my friend
When she came for a cup of sugar.
The other neighbours became related
By exchanging coffee powder.
Now, apart from the T.V., books and my house
I have friends in the next street and beyond.
Giving or taking for free is not beggary
They can be the beginning of
Happy relationships too.
Despite language differences
I have a lot to speak about now.

*Translated by V. Padma*

## ILAMPIRAI

### *Amma*

You,
who abandoned me,
without a lullaby
to toil in the forest,
even as I screamed and wept...
Afraid that I would turn fair
if you bathed me with soap,
you lay me down in a heap of forest dirt...
You,
who nagged me and
dragged me off to the fields,
even before I turned ten:
'Will they give money or what,
if you go to school? You, who don't even have
a cloth for your waist, what good is education to you?
Just come, girl, to the fields.'

You, who asked me to blow out the lamp, saying:
'If you study for hours on end,
where will I go for kerosene?
Exams, exams, you say,
adding to my woes.'

You said
when I asked for exam fees:

'What sin have I committed
sending you to school?'
Lamenting thus, you grudgingly gave me
Rupees five.

You,
who gathered thorns to be sold,
barefoot yourself,
just so you could buy cheap slippers for me,
all because you saw me struggle
as I walked barefoot.

You,
who said,
so as to deflect despair
when the roof leaked from heavy rains
in the month of *aipasi:*
'Just summer rain. It will cool things down. Let it rain.'

You,
who asked eagerly, on top of everything, in '93 itself:
'A thing called aeroplane, it seems.
I believe it can fly.
Should one jump down straight?
Should one stand and fly?'

O mother,
who gave birth to me,
your daughter who's been to school

now writes lyrics and sings . . .
You,
who live in my heart,
better know this:
wherever I wander,
my first song will always be for you —
from the depths of my very being,
a lullaby . . .

*Translated by Subashree Krishnaswamy and K. Srilata*

## MALATHY MAITRI

### *Nest*

Man and wife
managed to build a home
running from pillar to post.
On the branch of the coconut tree
northwards, with much cooing,
they even hatched an egg.
In a few days,
now and then a fledgling peeped out,
shrilly cheeping, exposing its red throat.

Birds grow up in no time at all.

The fledgling emerges from the nest,
grooms its feathers,
flitting from branch to branch.

You ought to witness the first flight.

For some days now
I've been watching the tree.
Today the bird seems full of life,
bustling about, leaping here and there.
Sitting down, it flaps around,
again and again.

In a flash
it unfurls its wings and flies,
perching on the terrace wall.

As children, we climbed trees,
destroyed nests,
stole green pebble-eggs
to fry and eat.

Inside our stomachs
who knows how many crows there are
wings spread,
waiting.

*Translated by K Srilata and Subashree Krishnaswamy*

## SUGIRTHA RANI

### *Amma*

I call out to you
in a voice
full of life.
Your cheeks,
once like freshly plucked flowers
have withered now,
and your silence,
you guard it like the music
of a protected forest.
I offer at your feet
my first poem that
tumbled out,
a newborn
covered in sticky blood.
With my wet hair
I wipe your cracked feet,
but you pull away.
I have crushed
the dreams that lay buried
deep in you,
I know.
But what to do,
writing is work for me,
like your making tea and snacks.

Like bees dusting off pollen
with careless ease,
I leave you
and this village
enveloped by hills.
Somewhere, a bird
that looks like you
calls out loud.

*Translated by Subashree Krishnaswamy and K Srilata*

## UMA MAHESWARI

### *Barren Plants*

Say something!
Say something about
the unlaundered shirt,
the tasteless sambar,
even if you don't discuss
literature, cinema and the like.
Say something about
a new face you saw today,
an unexpected incident,
a kolam unsmudged
despite vehicles trampling over it,
a marketing gimmick,
reflections of a plant that hasn't flowered —
say something, can't you!
Give life to memories crushed
by the weight of days.
When I try to trap the sunlit dust
filtering in through the window
or
the moon in a bowl of water,
smile at me,
or . . . call me a fool.
Apologise right now
for hurriedly snatching your hand away

when I held it to my womb
filled with child
just so you could feel the flutter.
Before you fling my sari away,
savour the flowers
buried in its folds.
When next
you weigh me down at night,
ask —
why I stare at the coconut tree
swaying outside the window.

*Translated by K Srilata and Subashree Krishnaswamy*

## VATSALA

### *Why didn't I become a poet?*

It's only after you asked me
that I wondered
why I never became a poet.

Digging deep,
I found no evidence
that I wasn't one.
I'd like to ask you something:
do dead poems count?
Since they dissolved
while still unborn
I couldn't give them shape.
I wasn't aware of their inception,
so I never recorded their time of birth.

But, with some, their time of death
is clear to me now.

One died when my grandmother praised
the neat way I folded the clothes.
A couple when
I picked up the ladle,
sorry for my mother
who struggled with my brothers' voracious greed
and my father's fastidious tongue.

A few passed away when
I befriended a typewriter
to save up for a gold chain,
just so a yellow thread could be tied
round my neck.

Bored, are you?
I will keep it short then.
A hundred vanished as I
washed my babies' bottoms,
tutored my darling children,
saved up for my son's overseas education,
stood by my husband as he washed the feet
of the son-in-law from America.
If they all come to life and take shape,
a poet I will be.

If not, next month
after his death anniversary,
when my greencard darlings go back home,
after my numb feelings are massaged and
I journey a bit into my eyes
and release my breath completely
who knows,
I might become a brand new poet.

*Translated by K Srilata and Subashree Krishnaswamy*

# GUJARATI

## SAROOP DHRUV

### *'I'*

I am a resolution to survive
I am an incarnation of the imperishable autograph

In the mirrors of words
I am an extension of myself

Here I am, as strong as a foundation
A root, a base; like grammar.

Revolt flows constantly in my veins
I am an eternally bleeding wound.

I am in search of the self
I am a moment of explosion.

*Translated by the poet*

### *Letter to Taslima*

It's your head they want, Taslima,
isn't it,
your head?
How can they know
that our wrists, our fingers,

our pens, our punching fists
                are all?
There's nothing else, nothing.
Tell the dolts this trunk,
even this headless trunk,
will
still
strain and fight
and write and write and write . . .

*Translated by the poet*

## *Beyond the Flapdoor*

For what I want to tell you,
I cannot find the words.
The wretched words have become the flapdoor of the family
  room*
And I am repelled by the sight
Of the rabbit's feet peeping under the fence.
I feel a peculiar sensation below my navel
At the sound of the tender carrot
Crunched by sharp nails and tiny teeth
And I can't stop what's happening.
Because when the thousand-armed one**
Is providing the nine hundred ninety-ninth garment
Before him he sees the luscious sugarcane glimmering.
And although he knew all about it
When the waiter went to wipe the tables this morning

He saw that
Between the rings made by the glasses on the table
In the midst of the field thick with sugercane
Lay a half-length sari and an anklet . . .
Now you tell me!
If I want to tell you this, is there any way I can?

*Translated by Shirin Kudchedkar*

* In old restaurants there is often a separate little room where a family or a couple can sit in privacy behind half-doors commonly known as 'flapdoors'.

** The 'God who provides for all' is often referred to in Saurashtra as 'He with the thousand arms'.

## SANSKRITIRANI DESAI

### *What do You Think?*

Regularly
The guillotine of the horizon
chops down the day,
and the sun,
a severed head,
tumbling, rolls away from the trunk.
Surely the goddess is pleased:
a perfect day
With *32 lakshanas**
offered up daily
by the ringing guillotine.
So many offerings
over thousands of years
and what has come of them?
So then . . .
are the sacrificial rites not right?
or the world unworthy of redemption?
Or the sun short of *32 lakshanas*?

*Translated by Rita Kothari and the poet*

* *32 lakshanas* refers to a person possessing the 32 qualities of the perfect man.

## PANNA NAIK

### *Snapshot*

Today I'm happy
Why I cannot tell.
Can this joy
be photographed, framed,
and hung upon
a bedroom wall?

*Translated by Rita Kothari and the poet*

## MANISHA JOSHI

### *Birth*

On the distant end of the pond at the
town's outskirts
A sandpiper cries out, shrill
And a wearied crane stands still, one leg up,
having fathomed the lake's smooth surface
at a glance.

Nor are these waters, anymore, secret
and deep.

Not knowing any of all this, they are coming
from far off.

The flamingoes journeying in many boats
How now to stop them?

There are indeed some isles

— a few large, dry rocks—
should flamingoes be disembarked
and halted there?

Where there is a fragrance of the oil
of dead tortoises,

The ash of the sea-shell,
expensive medicinal marine plants
The use of which is completely unknown yet

And water-lillies grown in the whirlpools
And left on the isles by the seagulls
all unblossomed and deep-red.

— and suppose the flamingoes stay on there ever after?

*Translated by Sitanshu Yashaschandra Mehta*

## *Re-Birth*

The flamingoes are dead. What next?
The phoenix has turned into ashes.

And it's not yet a hundred years since
and on the heap of these ashes
a pup is making himself comfortable.

The sweep of phoenix wings is seen
in the pup's flapping, hanging ears
Its tiny little twisting tail.

—That is the phoenix's soul.

Its teeth chewing upon a bone: Those
are his full span of life.

And all the foresight
of the phoenix's flight high above the sea
is become the flaring nostrils of the pup

alerted by the smell of leather.

On the ash-heap of the phoenix
The pup has gone to sleep
Of the feel of limbs, inside the ashes
Its dreams are made.

It's not going to wake up, never
Its thoughts are all that is left of his
liquid virility in those ashes.

From those no phoenix shall be born — none.

*Translated by Sitanshu Yashaschandra Mehta*

# MALAYALAM

## ANITHA THAMPI

### *Afterwards*

Burnt out
cigarette stubs
will grow back
attach themselves to the lip
And ask for fire

Fallen strands of hair
Will rewind themselves
Into oiled, shining plaits
And ask for flowers

In the night
Which seeps from the nerves
And spreads out like dirt,
Dreams
Lie close to each other
Thirsting for water

In the land where fire has not been invented
In a sandscape that has never seen flowers
We will keep searching
Till dawn
For that little shard of red
For us to think —

Fire, for you
Flower, for me.

*Translated by C.S. Venkiteswaran*

## VIJAYALAKSHMI

### *Making of a Soup*

Certainly anyone can make a soup.
Tomatoes, onions, green chillies,
Black pepper, flakes of garlic and salt.
Near the hot hearth
Sweating.

It will take a while to cook.
Must be careful when stirring.
Lumps should not form.
Don't forget
The fragrance of cut coriander leaves.

After that we sit around the table.
Four guests, sunk in four different trains of thought.
Four escapees, four past mistakes.
As croutons we add to the soup
Our great dreams, the ones we are not able to get rid of.
We are waiting for the soup to cool.

The enticing warmth of the soup,
Its attractive red tint,
Four guests, sunk in four different trains of thought.
Four new steps into coming days.

Now we are starting to eat the soup.
On red horses we cross the
Deserts of empty stomachs.
Perhaps we are no more just four.

Behind us there stretches
A vast multitude of faceless ones
Asking for soup.
From four to forty, to four hundred, four thousand,
Forty thousand, four lakhs.
The multitude grows and grows.
Like the endless dreams of the hopeful.

Certainly we can improve upon the soup.
By adding to it
Love, commitment, hope, dreams,
And our never-ending labour of love.

*Translated by T.K. Ramachandran*

## *The Beast Trainer*

I fear you.

Your eyes,
the contorted dance of whips
hoops that smite
twirl on your fingertips.
But maybe there's tenderness
in your bosom?
Nevertheless,
let me confess,

I fear you.

This frame trembles
for the jungle, and yet
moist eyes stay rapt
on this fiery circlet.
Leap I must,
with my eyes shut!
How hard, how long
I trained, but
against the leash
the mirage strains,
in fitful wrestling
with its chains.

Behind the bamboo grove

The black boulder stands
And crouched above
I see below
the spring shines
with bands of black and gold
and my face, rare, grand, feline!

Cool curdled moonlight, a
leafy pavilion gently
beckons my love.
Tender growls, sweetly
laden moments, blessed rest
the murmur, the music
of little ones at play
A split second, and then
The whip rises to flay.
the strike, lightning-sharp.

No, no, desist, the flaming eyes
the stinging words,
the body burns, as
pride crumbles to shards.
I growl, in silence:

I fear you.

Do not rub me down
With the harsh eye
Of Stone Man,

a beast, yes, I am
But no way can I stay
behind these bars.
It's crushing the prey
beneath my feet,
piercing the flesh
with pointed teeth
that make me brim with content,
lust for the kill,
for jets of blood
upon my face
in steady flood.
Many are those
who sit in rows,
It's them I wish,
I ache, to gore.

Answer me:
How can a beast be just a toy?
A mere slave, he,
when crushed, when tamed.
But time to time, within my core
a wild ancestor
rises to roar.
The ancient one,
lord of leafy heights
he who vaults above the sky
to snatch away the daystar bright.

Lowered, my eyes
beneath his gaze
my body tires
before his grimace
I bow, how can I not
salute his fearsome grace.

No, do not look long
at the blinding brilliance
of his form
it shatters the eyes,
the intent gaze,
rather, let these claws
gouge the eyes out of my face.

No, that can't be!

Fear, fear alone, fills
my slavish heart.
Bend I will
for the whip to crack
and to leap into your fiery well
Stay awake, I will, I will.

*Translated by J. Devika*

## LALITHA LENIN

### *Ignorance*

Moving among ants
with an olfactory nerve
I didn't sense I had a mind.
So
I didn't look
for a mirror among them.

Sporting and chatting
Among swallows
I didn't realise
I didn't have a tail.
So
I didn't reach the poolside
to jump with
full-grown frogs.

Buried deep
in the lines of writers,
I didn't learn
from where
those quills
shed drops of blood.

With a heart out of place,
I walked

with my head held high.
Getting used
to curing heartaches for heartburn
and heartburns for heartache,
I didn't know
what to do
for pain in the heart!

With no clue
about the price of
my children's limbs
or their market value,
I posed as an ignorant mother.
I don't know why
on meeting the doctor
I was reminded of the assassin
and on seeing the assassin,
I remembered the saviour.

Without recognising
the leeward of leaves
and windward of waves,
as an ant
I lie trampled beneath someone's foot
with an insight
gobbling up the universe,
a stare
lying unshaken.

*Translated by Annie George*

## *Lesson One: Shakuntala*

Dushyanth
preserved love letters
not in lotus leaves
but in the heart!
Read
not in lines
but on lips
of silence!
Even then
I fail
to understand you
or you me
and therefore we get no deliverance
from this mystical communion.

In the forest
where lovers lose their way
in aimless wandering,
the dazed doe runs
from the hunter's eye.
The Karuka grass and death fleet
its birthright.
The love secret
in the rolling dew
on blades of grass
in the gathering chill
escaping the sun's thirst

is yet unknown.
The startled looks
try to trace
the origin of the bee-song
that spreads across
the river Malini,
the wind
and the meadows.

Not familiar with
the radiance
of blinking stars
or an active voice
enlightened only when it meets
words of romance.
The creator
gathers them
in his arms
and gives life to
Lesson one: Shakuntala.
Converting
experience to ecstasy
and enigma to expression
she keenly awaits
Decrees.

*Translated by Annie George*

## ROSE MARY

### *What I have to tell you*

You
must not fear my love,
It expects nothing from you.

You
should not mistrust my friendship.
It does not wish to own you.

Once upon a time,
on a dark, dark night
the spirits came
and stowed away in my heart
a hoard of love.
That gift was given
while I was asleep.
When I awoke,
love surged over the
banks of my heart.
The sad, the lonely
came to snatch it away.
Love stayed full, though.
I poured it into goblets.
I wandered
beneath the boundless sky,
across vast open spaces,

through deserted waysides.
I held in my hands
the overflowing goblet.

You
should feel not guilty
about my love;
I do not hold out to you
what I took back from another;
have I not told you
of the love that withers unfelt,
of the goblet that brims over?

I want to make some things
clear.
If you come to me some day
do not assume the gestures
of the king
who goes to meet his slave.
I do not need rent-free land,
or provinces to rule.
Do not wear the mien
of a god
before his devotee.
I have no boons
to ask of you.
My soul is not arid
that it should be filled
with your radiance.

Like one emperor to another,
like one friend to another,
come to me
as an equal.
Like a flute
pursuing the tune,
like the question
seeking its answer,
may your steps be
as light
and as carefree . . .

*Translated by J. Devika*

## *The Mask*

Look,
henceforth we need
shed our tears
only in easy stages.
Won't our faces
turn bleak, pallid,
with crying that shatters the heart?

From now on
Let's have friendships light and fluffy.
Won't love that's too intense
lay waste the marrow?

Hereafter, let's board small canoes

and paddle
along the usual channels.
What if we lose our bearings,
daring farther and farther shores
seduced by the call of unknown seas?

Henceforth,
let there be light handshakes;
think what will happen
if our masks shrivel and fall
in an ardent embrace

And what if we fall back, flustered,
quivering,
as the heart's naked valleys,
the blood-spurting sores,
flash past our eyes?

And then, what if we,
blinded to each other,
have no other way
but to flee,
heads bowed,
our faces hidden by pale hands?

*Translated by J. Devika*

## SAVITHRI RAJEEVAN

### *The Slant*

This slanting light at four o'clock.
On the tiled roof,
with the eye of a palmist
the cawing crow, head aslant.

Alongside the crow
its shadow also sits —
sits at a slant.

In the courtyard
like a trembling hand
the slanting shadow of the coconut frond.
In my room
the thin shadows of the window bars,
they too lie aslant.

Outside the gate
a stranger walking along
the sound of his footsteps —
why is it slanted?
the forecast of the crows
the soughing of the sea-breeze
the footsteps of the passerby —
why are they slanted?
I've become suspicious.

Finally,
on my table
on its own axis
I saw the earth slant
but I sit straight
in front of it.

On this slanting earth
where everything is slanted
Why is it
I alone am straight?

*Translated by Ayyappa Paniker and Arlene Zide*

## *Krishna*

Krishna —
how should I love him?
He has mothers
More than one —
Yasoda, Devaki,
Then Pootana and Kalindi
cows and cows and
flowers and flowers
All of them mothers to him.

Krishna —
how should I love him?
His fathers

more than one —
Vasudeva and Nada and
Brahma and Yama
Incarnations,
then unincarnations,
All these fathers to him.

Krishna —
how should I love him?
His loves too
not one,
many —
Bhama, Rukmini,
then Radha and Meera,
sixteen thousand and eight girlfriends,
kids, all
girls, all
friends to him.

Krishna —
how should I love him?
As the breeze, moving
as the mind, still
as the peacock's plume,
as sweet sound,
as deluge,
leaf floating
on deluge,
as buttermilk pail,

Or else
as the poet, with song flowing.
Which way should I love him?

As a foe, valiant
as a friend, chariot-borne
as devotion, as detachment,
as sculpture, as stone
as night, moon's riverbed
as fear, as shade —
Or else
a cuckoo, the source of song
By which tune should I love him?

Krishna —
how should I love him?
cloud-shade on the skin
yellow clothing on the body
lotus-petal in the eye
love in the mind
and
a curse on the head —
Which arrow should I love him by?

Or else,
Krishna —
why should I love him?

*Translated by Udaya Kumar*

# MARATHI

## AMITA KOKATE

### *One should take*

One should take
One complete canvas
On one's body
Christ's smile, the Buddha's eyes
Krishna's blue colour, Radha's love
And Meera's destiny
And many such things
One should put into the collage
But one should pour into it
Only one's own heart
And one's own feet of clay
After all
These are the things
One needs on the roads of fate

*Translated by Sachin Ketkar*

## MALIKA AMAR SHEIKH

### *Venus*

She doesn't have arms
Like me

Her vision utterly dead
She stands in a showcase
Frozen stiff
Like me

With difficulty,
She manages to cling
To the rocky robes of culture
Between her legs
And stony lips
Closed tight
Like me

Women in the cities melt
Turn into statues of Venus
A primeval woman
Lets out a stony scream
The city collapses
At her feet
Throwing the sky
In disarray.

*Translated by Sachin Ketkar*

## *A Poem for a Dali Painting*

These refusals
Scattered everywhere
These faces
Pouring out of words
This dead eyelash

*Everything is arid*

Even then, time is still alive
Resting on it
Dali's watch still elongages
The tongue of time
Soaked and squirming
Even then
How come these black and red ants of desire

*Are still alive*

Who is alive?
Time? Or is it us? Or is it this shapeless space?
This throbbing of breath
Or are we listening to the ticking of this watch

*Primitive millions of years ancient*

What is behind that huge eyelid?
A watch

A moment  a silence
Or a dead tear?

*Translated by Sachin Ketkar*

## *Metropolis*

A total woman
Complete with a womb

A complete monsoon
A complete winter
A sky and a shore

In her breasts and thighs
You seek the meaning of the world
Or seek the answers to your questions
Or amusement or change.
Wife, mistress and whore
What is the difference between these?
Only of numbers . . .

But there is more to them
Than the body
Which you deliberately rebuff . . .
Really,
Is bed an answer to all the questions?
When you turn away after sex
You are not even aware whether

The one sleeping next to you
Is a woman or graveyard or dung
In such circumstances
I am dolefully surprised
You can speak of poetry
This garrulous living
These false crowns
How long would you do
With these toys of feelings?
Your boats
After going round women's thighs
Raise their sails
And head towards some destination
Women say after waving handkerchiefs of wombs
'Let the poor fellow find his island.'
Then they become the third shore
Or you land on their nipples
And cry, 'America, America! Eureka, eureka!'
Or something of the sort
When the seas of her hair surge
You hang your bodies
On her lips and eyelashes
To dry
Your bonfires of delicious overcooked debates
You feel overjoyed, overwhelmed, satisfied . . .
I never said she would be godlike
But it is necessary for you to cover
Your half-naked souls with her!

*Translated by Sachin Ketkar*

## KAVITA MAHAJAN

### *A Doubt*

She never quite understood
When the termite turned up in the house
Along with the big fat book.
Her sight was fixed on the letters
Of the old rare volume
She had bought from the footpath.
She did not notice
The dark spots near the letters.
The termite continued to spread
Through old and new books,
Through the cupboard
Along with the books,
Not limiting itself to cupboards
It spread all over the house,
Groping for doors and windows
Like the meaning of caged letters
It spread all over the mind...

The Master as such
Had disliked the idea
Of bringing books
That too from the footpath
Into the house
To fritter away money like this
After printed letters, papers and rags . . .

Now it was the termite
Which revealed the weakness
Of wood, bricks and cement.
It was bringing down
The foundation of all those things
Thought to be well built,
Resilient and enduring!

*Translated by Sachin Ketkar*

## *Depraved*

My flesh
Soft
Like the deep yellow petals
Of a sunflower
Showing off openly
The seductive seeds
Of the dark black sin
However hard you may clutch
At the roots
As much as you may nourish me
So that I survive
—I am definitely obliged
Master for that—
But I can't take off
My depraved eyes
From the sun.

*Translated by Sachin Ketkar*

## *Modest*

Women with masters
Avoid
Women without masters . . .
The first thing when they see one of them
They adjust their kumkum
Check their mangalsutra with their hands
Weighed down with matrimonial bangles;
Cover their entire being with a modest palloo.

As they pass by
Avoiding her
They cast a stealthy glance at her
And also at their masters
Who are looking at her . . .

Their steps automatically hurry
Towards their respective
Secure
Cages.

*Translated by Sachin Ketkar*

## PRADNYA LOKHANDE

### *Even this agony is not mine*

Even this agony is not mine alone
I am talking of time present
Clinging on to these roots

Even this clay is not mine alone
I am talking of time past
Centuries layered upon centuries
On this terrain is chiselled
Ever modern bare blazing shadow
I am talking of time future.

May my fidelity remain unflinching
To this colossal striving
To compassion's streaming
To my gender's simmering.

*Translated by Rajeev Kalelkar*

# TELUGU

## KONDEPUDI NIRMALA

### *Synonym for a Heart*

Not so suddenly, you see
gradually, like
moisture under a mat
that twelfth year
creeps up on you unawares
your body lengthening softening
transparent as a glass jar
centres a vague fear
while your tremulous downward gaze
is arrested by
twin exclamation marks

fluidly flanking
the silken cleft of your bosom
smooth as a banana leaf
neither solid nor liquid
the real synonym for a heart!

Now you can seize it in your palm
those tiny twin hillocks
tipped crimson
like a hennaed fingertip
pointing to the moon
silent jasmine buds
quivering slightly as you walk

bathing when you bathe
sleeping when you sleep
and shadowing your waking moments

Indifferently  cushioning each glance
with neither distaste nor desire
longing
folded hands frozen
in greeting
drenched in the heat of that beauty
tremulous with longing
folded hands frozen in greeting
mesmerised
like frozen waves or melting sculptures
now no longer in control
they burst forth like two miraculous globes
shrinking from each passing glance
in a movement of revulsion
like prisoners of war
shrouded in silence
Now striving for motherhood
in rigorous penance they
grow onerous with dignity
drooping slightly
like a neck weighted by garlands
asking
is love dark or light.
Now in the summer of the middle years
When the shadow of doubt

lengthens and haunts you
your heart sinks
to the sound of 'Hush, you know nothing'
and to hide your shrinking heart
your voice grows louder
your words inconsequential
fumbling at your glasses with
your sari edge
you can no longer tell the difference
between suffering and pleasure
moving like a patchwork quilt
and in the final analysis
if you set aside the ex gratia gifts
the Kanchi silks, the gold moon necklace
what is left save that
thickening line of darkness
skirting your blouse
circling your waist
coming to rest on your heart
disappearing, startled by discovery
At sixty
trapped by time
wasted by disease
worn out by bitter reality
as if my guts had been ripped out
to garland my neck
the dark veins stain
my skin
my juices dry

welcoming death and resignation
in the same moment
your breasts lie flat as veined betel leaves
bearing a dried black betel nut
indescribably pensive
patient  piteous

*Translated by Vasanth Kannabiran*

## *This Side of the Edge of Day*

That it is night
is the only reason.
That it is night
is the only justification.
To drive the night
to the edge of daybreak
is a necessity.
Here
the twining of four hands
is no embrace
with eternal accusations
and egos never submerged
even for a moment
with disbelief
as if even dying let alone living
Is not for one's self
raising a voice only in argument
each step pointing to parting ways

and the sound of cracked time
a bone gnawed by a pup
a bullock harnessed to a mill
unable to break the seeing of signs
unable to capture the heat of love
we are defeated
I try bitter truths
you try vanishing minutes
drenched in the sweat
of that defeat
we claim as victory
not a teardrop to recover
stricken shy shameless
because you cannot switch on a glow
you use soap, creams and powder
burying your head in haste
and those flowers incense and coins
that signal every occasion
ignite the surroundings
and the hoarse weariness of those
fractured crevices of the heart
moist hope sobbing at
the venom of words.
And we slither snakelike
with borrowed faces and desires.

That it is night
is the only criterion
That it is night

is the only justification
And silence
crushed by roaring landslides
over the caves of day
and the path of unwisdom
spread between life and living
one must tie up the night
before the edge of daybreak.

*Translated by Vasanth Kannabiran*

## GHANTASALA NIRMALA

### *Jugal Bandhi*

The lamp is extinguished
The magic of darkness conjures forth
smoky dreams
Inhibitions bloom in the
intimacy of solitude
glowing red-tipped fragrant welcoming
as incense.
Reddened eyes raw as wounds
filled with anxiety during the day
healed and soothed by the
balm of darkness
turn into pools of moonlight
shedding
the robes of decency
soaked and heavy
with the flood of
daily rituals of respect
striving to submerge in desire
twin souls turning into
synonyms of shamelessness
as the senses ripple
singing to the touch of fingers
on stretched strings
the tinkle of soft laughter
sends desire welling into the

melody of Megh Malhar
an ancient ray of desire
strikes in the darkened stream
and twin lotuses cast forth
the fragrance of fulfilment
the body trembling as it
peaks to pleasure
the fingers spinning secrets
together begin to unravel
the gordian knot
breaths and sighs turn
to ropes of flowers
swinging the heart to
the heights of ecstasy
the jugal bandhi
embodied voices matching note for note
rise to unimagined heights
blood swelling forth intoxicated
deeped secrets shared released
fulfilled diamonds of sweat sparkle
as they catch the light.

The palanquin must stop
after all this the swing of delight must cease
That wisp shawl of pleasure cannot cover
the nakedness of body and soul
That sudden spreading fragrance
evaporates in a fire
eyes search frantic

for those silken dreams
clumsily dropped by unskilled hands
and that soft silvery mirror of moonlight
gently reflecting fineness and flaw
as perfection turns dim
and the anti-climax of reality
returns to confront you
problems like raw sores
truths like redhot coals
as questions burn again
and the smell of burning flesh
rises from the innermost soul
and the hanging thread of ash from the
incense stick
Is the last witness
the heart that glowed with pride
a moment ago cracks
the gem of delight turns into a lump of clay
the flow of the dark cool night is
pierced by the first cruel ray.

*Translated by Vasanth Kannabiran*

## VOLGA

### *Spring will not Come*

No more will spring come to this town.
Wheat sprouts may bloom again in fields
wearing small, tiny ears
but spring will not come here again.
Men will take birth and go around
they'll weep and they'll laugh,
but spring will not come here again.
Unpolluted wind blowing
Crossing the smell of charred flesh
butterflies flying in soft sun
pigeon-wings flapping to warm rays —
spring will not look in here again.
Except for freezing cold or scorching sun
As *mandaras* bloom
to this town blossoming death
spring at least will not come.

Upon charred bodies
boils of distrust erupt oozing pus
but here no trees wear buds.
As the singing birds were flung into flames
through closed windows slits
and the moans floated unrestrained
to the mango buds blooming here

*koels* do not open their throats.
Here where blood-red *mandaras* bloom
spring at least will not come.

*Translated by Vasanth Kannabiran*

## VIMALA

### *The Kitchen*

I remember the kitchen's
flavour upon flavour
a mouthwatering treasury,
pungence of seasonings
and the aroma of incense
from the prayer room
next door. Each morning
the kitchen awoke
to the swish of churning butter,
the scraping of scoured pots.
And in the centre, the stove,
fresh, washed with mud, painted
and bedecked, all set to burn.

We saved secret money in the
seasoning box; hid sweets too,
and played at cooking with lentils and jaggery.
We played Mother and Father
In the magic world of a kitchen
That wrapped childhood in its spell.

No longer playground for the grown-up girl
now trained into kitchenhood.
Like all the mothers and mothers' mothers

before her
she becomes woman right here.

Our kitchen is a mortuary
Pans, tins, gunny bags
Crowd it like cadavers
That hang amid clouds of damp woodsmoke.
Mother floats, a ghost here,
A floating kitchen herself,
her eyes melted in tears,
her hands worn to spoons,
her arms spatulas that turn
into long frying-pans and
other kitchen tools.

Sometimes Mother glows
like a blazing furnace
and burns through the kitchen
pacing, restless, a caged tiger,
banging pots and pans.
How easy, they say,
The flick of a ladle and the cooking's done.
No one visits now.
No one comes to the kitchen
Except to eat.

*Translated by Vasanth Kannabiran*

## SHAHJAHANA

### *Lift that Veil*

In childlike innocence
I laughed and reached
for the bright coloured pleats
of the curtain hanging on the door
little knowing that was the
first chain on freedom's wings.
When a similar veil
stretched across my mother's face
I little grasped the weight of that curse on life's dream
how much despair gathers
how many dreams are slaughtered
behind each veil
how many desires
how many hopes
lie smashed behind dark veils
where life is imprisoned behind a veil
where mighty banyans of mad orthodoxy flourish
stamping women down the more they suffer
just lift that veil gently and look upon
those gulmohars scattering
the light of freedom
my sisters who have never known
the taste of moonlight
or raindrops or springtime
ever . . .

*Translated by Vasanth Kannabiran*

# CHALLAPALLI SWAROOPA RANI

## *Wild Flower*

When has my life been truly mine?
In the home male arrogance
Sets my cheek stinging
While on the street caste arrogance
Splits the other cheek open . . .

Chasing the faraway distant hope
of an education
Reaching the shore of the hostel
Shrinking from the hungry look of
the warden
I long to gather my body into
a fist and fling it into the distance . . .

Good enough to fulfil lust
but not good enough for a
family

I feel like hiding my face
in a stream.

*Translated by Vasanth Kannabiran*

## RAVULAPALLI SUNITHA

### *Suicide is My Protest*

Unable to bear
the gentleness of my husband
who softly spreads firewood
and stones
on my petal-soft heart
I set myself ablaze.
That then is my protest.

To escape the
wolves that would
roast and eat me
I lay my head on the lap
of the husband
who cooks and consumes me
and burn myself.
That then is my protest.

Like a globule of spit
collected and spat
in the face of this justice
that chokes my very breath
I tighten the noose
around my neck.
That is the only protest I know.

These tears and anger
smashed against
this world that will not let me grow
and this time that will not let me live
is my fearful protest.

This my death
a resounding slap
in the face of your values
and this my dying declaration —
did it reach you?

*Translated by Vasanth Kannabiran*

## VASANTH KANNABIRAN

### *Asmita*

When did I realise
what it was to be a woman?
was it
as I blossomed forth
at fifteen
followed by lingering glances
and lustful looks
and walked forth
tall and proud borne
on that tide of desire that
cradled me wherever I went
Or was it when his lips met mine
in a soul-searching kiss
that sent heaven and earth
spinning
Was it when
pulsing to his desire
my body exploded
in a series of rockets
lighting the sky
like frenzied fireworks
even as a chain of orgasms
blew my body into raining atoms!
Was it perhaps
when I swelled with child

and my whole being
centred around this new creature
rooted miraculously in my womb
Wasn't it when with a shriek of pain
I pushed him forth into the world
at last
covered with blood and slime
to hear the walls echo
for unto us a son is born
Was it when
cradled in my arms
his tiny fists clutching
my swollen breast
he gobbled his milk
eyes closed and content
was it when
my body racked by disease
exploding in pain
stilling my screaming mind
I smiled
spreading calm
emanating comfort
Wasn't it rather
when I began
to stretch the sinews of my mind
ponder on these untruths
as I began to peel off
layer after layer
of illusion

saying not this
not this
and no
not this
When I began to see myself
enclosed
defined
by not this
dared to look nothingness in the face
dared to dwell
in a vacuum
risk being erased
altogether
to re-centre my existence
that I realised what it meant
to be a woman.

*Translated by the poet*

# HINDI

## ANAMIKA

### *Women*

They read us
casually
like one reads the torn pages
of a child's notebook
before it is made into paper-cones
for *chanajorgaram*

They looked at us
crossly
as one looks, half-asleep, at the alarm clock
when it rings too early
in the morning.

They listened to us
distractedly
as one listens to filmi songs
on cheap cassettes
in a crowded bus.

They suffered us
absently
like one suffers, barely, the distant pain
of a relative
far away.

One day we said
we're human, too
read us carefully
one word at a time
as you would a job advertisement
after your B.A.

Look at us with yearning
as, shivering, you would look at a fire
                    out of reach.

Listen to us
as you would the soundless void
and try to understand, slowly,
                    a language newly learned.

As soon as they heard this
                    out of nowhere
                    like a locust-horde
                    wild rumours, screeching
'Women without character
spreading like weeds
Egged on by the misguided
women with no virtue
well-bred and bored
vagabond  self-indulgent
whiling away their time with idle verse . . .'

Then with sidelong glance
with mocking gesture
'And even this poetry is not theirs.'

The rest is dismissal.

O blessed Fathers
O men of eminence
we beseech you
spare us
                this attention.

*Translated by Ritu Menon*

## *Unemployed*

Nowadays I just read ancient scripts —
Indus Valley Civilisation's ancient script and the rest
I read them little by little.
Every language is the language of pain —
ever since I've understood this
in whichever language it might be written
I can sort out the alphabets.
In my infinite emptiness
this is the only thing that I've done
in the whirlpool of every pain
I've learnt their wobbly notations.
There is a fire in me, too —
this writes something

on the wind's frayed pieces
and then crumples it
throwing it beneath a broken cot.
Sometimes my mother opens and reads these pieces
and her spectacle-lenses fog up.
This is the exact point where my fire
perspires, turning to water.
My cuffed hands are impatient.
They want to do something.
In them, there is strength;
they can unearth a mountain and let
milk flow out as a stream.
They don't mind —
even after digging up a mountain
only a mole emerges.
Freckled and very cold
are my cuffed hands —
they haven't picked berries yet,
nor swept the earth bent over
tasting the earth's sweetness
till the very last.
Never has any tattered shawl
stretched in front of them
smilingly begging for such berries.
The moon is no longer that pale yellow —
there is a layer of dirt on its yellowness,
much like an overused torn notebook
barely bright, tired —
a notebook that wouldn't suffice for work

even for the miserliest bania.
Hey butterfly, tell me —
how far is the road's end
how far the last sigh's limitless desire?
'Desire' — which bird's name is that?
Has this bird ever
descended onto your courtyard
or perched on your hands?
Then why do people say —
a bird in hand
is worth more than two in a bush.
Wringing my hands
I often wonder —
are my hands
two flintstones?

*Translated by Sudeep Sen*

## *Salt*

Salt is earth's sorrow and its taste.
Earth's three-fourths is brackish water
and men's hearts a salt mountain.
Weak is salt's heart,
very quickly does it melt,
it sinks in shame
when plates are flung
due to salt's varied strength.
There stands

a government building
like a salt-shaker
shakes with much sophistication, sprinkles
salt in my wound.
Women are the salt of the earth
they have all the salt in the mould of their face.
Ask those women
how heavy they feel —
their saline faces
All those determined to pay the salt's price,
all those who couldn't betray their masters
have annoyed the seven seas and
the revolutionaries.
Gandhi knew the salt's worth
as the girl-guava-sellers.
Whether or not something
stays in the world
there shall always be salt.
God's tears and man's sweat —
this is salt
that balances the earth.

*Translated by Sudeep Sen*

## *The Door*

I was a door
The harder they beat me
The wider I opened

They walked in and saw
A great cosmic whirligig
When the grinding stops, the spinning begins
When the spinning stops, the sewing begins
Something or other, all day, non-stop.

And in the end my broom sweeps it all up
Sweeps up the stars in the sky
Mountains, trees, stones
All the shards and splinters of creation
Collects them in a basket
Stores them somewhere
                    deep inside
In some corner of the mind.

*Translated by Ritu Menon*

## *Untitled*

She entered her hotel room
Shook hands warmly
With her alone-ness
Pitch-dark the room was
Within her, too, pitch-dark
Like a well
The walls closed in around her
But no light switch
A wide open door
A faint light from the balcony
A waiter passing by
Came to her rescue
Chuckled as he offered the clue
'For light, Madam, shut the door.'
She shut the door firmly
And a thousand lights burned in the light bulbs
Like the thousand-petalled lotus of the Bodhisattva
Strange, she thought,
Why should closing a door
Make for light?

She stretched out on the bed
But felt her own chattai beneath her
Digging into her spine
Is every woman like the princess and the peapod?
So much to read
But she reached for the phone

Enquired about rates
Then, using up all her dollars,
Made three separate calls
The first to her children
'Hello, son
You dozed off as I packed.'

'Can't stop thinking of you'

'My most precious!'

The last two she said
Separately
To her anxious mother
And that sulking husband of hers.

Now, the cross-examination
God is her judge
How could she say
To three separate people
You are the most precious?
A complete deception.
Most precious is most precious
But the good lord set aside his pen and said,
'Woman that you are
You meant what you said.
For a woman all her dear ones
Are her dearest.'

*Translated by Ritu Menon*

## KSHAMA KAUL

### *They Threw Me Out*

First they threw me out of my home
And then my city
Again and again
I was ousted from the city where I took shelter.
They say I will be thrown out of this city too.

In each place I left behind
Grew the fruit I had planted
Haunted by my absence.
They say my spirit
                    spelt destruction.

Now I have a bag of seeds
All tied up
To lean my back against.

Spinning around me
Is the earth
So spinning,
Some day, my home will
                    spin into view again

And I will open my bundle
Never to tie it up again.

*Translated by Ritu Menon*

## GAGAN GILL

### *The Telephone and Silence*

Often we found ourselves crammed into a telephone booth. We would call those we barely knew. We would also call complete strangers. With bated breath we would imagine their homes, their appearance, what they might be doing at that moment. We would remain silent, since we couldn't ask such questions straight out.

A couple of days later, it would become a pattern. They didn't say, '*what the hell do you want?*' They would even listen intently to our absent voices. They would avoid slamming down the receiver on us. Sometimes, they would be caught waiting for our calls. So that we, who could not go into their homes, could make a place in their emptiness.

Till the very end they couldn't figure out if we'd come from another planet; that we didn't know what it was we wanted from them.

This is how we made our way through the alleys of the town. Only one rumour would filter through the whole bazaar. These days, it's the season of silence again on the telephone.

*Translated by Arlene Zide and the poet*

## *Days of the Dead*

In the days of the dead, sometimes our mothers would descend from the sky. We would make offerings to our fathers. We would send the aromas of various foods to the heavens. In the absence of our prayers, these mothers of ours would wander in the lower reaches of the sky. We didn't worry about their peace and believed that they wouldn't be in a hurry to find their own peace.

The fathers would take a long time to descend for the feast. It seemed they were at peace in the other worlds. When they'd finished, they'd glance at our worried faces with the same indifference they'd shown in life... We wouldn't serve our mothers, though they were right there next to our fathers.

We would wander restless for our peace; so would these mothers of ours. But we would offer libations of water only to our fathers.

*Translated by Arlene Zide and the poet*

## *Father*

Where her father is, poison dissolves in her blood. Many rats have died. Many centuries have gone off to sleep. They're both angry with themselves. Father and daughter.

Her eleven-year old father digs himself a grave. At thirty-six, she goes and lies down in it. Those women of the town, whom Father had called out to that day— *'I am here'*, won't go past.

*Translated by Arlene Zide and the poet*

## *Sialkot, 1947*

There is a train that always leaves. In it are crammed jittery people. Even in the toilets. No space anywhere even to squeeze in a sesame seed!

There are rioters on the outside. Carnage. Inside is a woman. And her embarrassment.

Till the end of the time, this incident recurs the same way, again and again. Two minutes before the train is supposed to leave, miserable, she gets off. This is the last time she'll be seen, looking for cover behind some bushes. Every day, between six and seven.

When trains no longer pass through this station.

*Translated by Arlene Zide and the poet*

## *Somebody Else's Love*

Sometimes somebody else's love would drift into our lives.

It might be an object found on the road which wasn't ours and hadn't been stolen by us. The temptation to keep it would abate after a while.

Often, after a little while, someone would come looking for it and take it away. Or it would itself tell us where it belonged and we would go and drop it back where it came from. It would turn up miraculously and leave.

To get over it, we would wait for some other love. And sometimes, we would even leave our own love behind at somebody else's door.

*Translated by Arlene Zide and the poet*

## *Letter*

The letter knocks at the door and you can't even open the latch of your solitude.
You've been locked in so long the latch has rusted.
You've been locked in so long you don't even know if you're caged from the inside or from out.

The letter knocks at the door and you say, from inside — please open the door outside. The letter probably can't hear your voice. And even if it does, can't figure out where the latch is.

Every despairing letter warns you, says, 'I won't come again.' Every non-answer dumps you back where you already were. No letter ever asks you, 'How did you get caged in like this in the first place?'

Every letter is sealed in an envelope of hope — and the envelope is torn.

*Translated by Arlene Zide and the poet*

## *The Fish – 1*

Death flashed in her eyes
As if it were a flickering star
As if it were a sky full of birds
As if it were the wind
Before it rains.

The fish lunged out of the water
As if
It were not death out there
But a longing to return
To the primal dream.

She caught the water
In her fine teeth
As if
It were the very last time
She knows, this river-fish
She'd die, going to the sea.

She wanted
Before this death of hers by drowning
One last time
To return
To the waters of the river.

Then, in her own waters
This river-fish
She drowned.

*Translated by J.P. Das, Madhu B. Joshi and Arlene Zide*

## *The Fish – 2*

It's not water
But the sky
Which has filled the brain of this fish.

Not water
But a longing to fly
Has filled the body of this fish.

She has been emptying herself
Into the sea
For centuries, endlessly.

Swimming past fish, large and small
Rapt in thought
This fish asks herself
Say, your sea, where has it gone?

Swimming, this fish
Repeats the question
As if it were a prayer or mantra.
She doesn't know, this fish

That the sky has filled her brain
That the skull-breaking rites
Have already begun
Within herself.

*Translated by J.P. Das, Madhu B. Joshi and Arlene Zide*

## RAJEE SETH

### *Mughal Garden*

We agree
The flowers are yours
The fruits are yours
The blades of lush grass are yours
The sentries are yours too.

We agree
That sky captured
within the four-sided courtyard is yours.
The wind that comes and knocks against its boundary walls
That's yours too.

But you need to know
The roots are ours
The nourishing compost
Is ours

> All the sunlight in that chunk of sky in your
> courtyard—
> that sky is ours
> the light is ours.

The water flowing down from the hills is ours
The wind carrying seeds is ours

All the rest of the earth
is ours.

*Translation by Arlene Zide and the poet*

## *Fear*

I was no historian
to be able to say
how the barbed wire sprang up
fencing off the open field.

The mosque wall, lying neglected
came up
overnight.
Who divided the narrow street
so quickly
right down the middle?
The thickets of creepers
covering the wall
were torn down.
The flowers of watchful light
hung
on lampposts
You hear everybody say—
the time of the Separatists has come.

A gate was plunked down
at the edge of the colony

two cement pillars
and a rattling chain

Who knows, this way
you may get to see
what's coming,
is almost never seen coming.

*Translated by Aruna Sitesh and Arlene Zide*
*in consultation with the poet*

## *It Can't Ever See — The Sky*

In the centre of the four-sided cementness of the wall
a window, fixed
Bars in the window
But, the window watches the sky —
its expanse of blueness.

The window watches
the play of the wind in every corner of the compass.
The window watches the infinite.
It's only the window which, unblinking
can see limitless skyness.

But the sky— it can't ever see
windowness.

*Translation by Arlene Zide and the poet*

## ARCHANA VERMA

### *Idol*

(1) First, the man was broken apart
and made into an idol
then that idol was broken apart
Thank goodness, the man
wasn't there
to see his idol being shattered.

(2) The smashing of idols goes on
They'll be set up again
Time and time again
they'll be recreated
Man is far more eager to be an idol
than be a man.

(3) How large and empty the *maidan* seems
even though it's packed with crowds
jam-packed
because there's no longer a statue.
They've all come together here again
to turn someone else into an idol.

(4) Idol-makers
don't know their own power
don't know anything else
except now and then how to rally on the *maidan*
don't know what happens

to that man
whose name they take
and raise their hands to
to take an oath
and go on to be martyrs
They don't know what happens to themselves either
when they knock down that statue
        smashing it to pieces.

        All they know is how to rally on the green field
        of the *maidan*.

*Translated by Arlene Zide and the poet*

## *Protection*

He planted a tiny sapling
and surrounded it with a fence
made of thorny branches.

It was the plant's own fault
that it grew up.
What else could the thorns do
but pierce it?

*Translated by Arlene Zide and the poet*

## *Man*

Water on a slope
will run downhill, they said
with an air of finality
That is, if water is water.
They didn't say: soil on a slope
if it's really soil
will soak up water
That a green carpet of grass
will sprout, covering the slope. It
may lie covering the slope, but
will turn its face skywards.
That is, if grass is really grass.

We're all standing on a slope. That
was the topic of discussion that evening. Water
can only flow downwards. This
was their conclusion. Trees
were not discussed at all. They may spring up
at the bottom of the slope, but
they grow upwards. The bigger
they grow, the easier
they're uprooted. That is, if trees
are really trees.

But the water
was not water. And the grass

wasn't grass either.   Or trees
trees.
But the topic wasn't water or grass or trees.
It was man,   about him
no one
said a word.

*Translated by Arlene Zide and the poet*

## *Watch*

Where today there is ice
long ago
there was a river.

There is a blank face
A frozen river.
An eye: a hole in the ice.
Just inside the opening
exists a world
imprisoned.
Utter darkness —
hard, terrifying, dense
keeps watch
on what goes on there.

A watch
on what once flowed in the veins of ice

The river
got through it all
by freezing.

*Translated by Arlene Zide and the poet*

## JYOTSNA MILAN

### *A Little Bit More*

Little by little
Every day she sinks
along with the sun
But the world
doesn't sink.
Not with her, not with the sun.
Then, every day, a little bit more,
she peeps out of the earth

She can be
anything
or every thing
at the same time —
from a leaf to a mountain

When was she a river?
Where was she?
When did she drown in the river?
When did she become the river?
Alongside a straw
it was her house floating
after she drowned.

*Translated by Aruna Sitesh and Arlene Zide*

## *Search*

Lights the gas
Makes tea
Cleans
the house
Changes the stained sheets
People come and say
          Your house
          looks
          like a real home

Surprised, she
looks around
her house
Goes from room to room
Searches for home
finds one room
sofa, settee, chairs
Another room, too
bedding, mats, machines
all these things
hemming her in
She's there in one of the rooms
and her soul
roams aimlessly
in search of home
as if it belonged to no one.

*Translated by Aruna Sitesh and Arlene Zide*

## *As If Never . . .*

She left
the house
as if
she were never going back

Didn't look back
maybe
the house would grab her
swallow her   maybe
follow crawling behind

Let it stay there
and do whatever it wanted
She
was up ahead
way up ahead
of herself.

*Translated by Aruna Sitesh and Arlene Zide*

## *Night*

Right from the start
in the inky dawn
the day begins for Ma
goes on
after everyone else's is done.

her nights
predictably short

and her days
predictably long
strike far into the night

no one thinks
it's her days
invading her nights.

Every day, she sleeps
with her legs drawn in

a crumpled-up Ma
in a left-over night

Her night not long enough
even to stretch her legs.

*Translated by Arlene Zide and the poet*

## *Back There*

Walking along
suddenly turned and looked
back
There was no street, no *maidan*
not that city
not those houses
not those places
not those people
From where she had started
there wasn't anything behind
back there
As if
someone had been wiping away
the life she had lived
moment
by moment.

*Translated by Aruna Sitesh and Arlene Zide*

## AMRITA BHARATI

### *Except in him*

When he looked inside for me
I'd be outside
and when he
looked for me outside
I'd go inside.
This is how the game got played
in the vale of Time.

Now I'm at the point
where from inside every door
opens out
and from outside
every door inwards.
I have no place to hide
except in him.

*Translated by Gagan Gill and Arlene Zide*

## *Blow*

A blow put a crack in the wall, [but] not in the heart
and it became a peephole between him and me
from where I could see him
                coming and going
                talking and laughing

This crack would widen
when I saw him sleeping —
and I'd see myself in the infinity of his closed eyes.

*Translated by Gagan Gill and Arlene Zide*

## *In This Cold Desert*

In this cold desert
not a single stream
no well

just dampness in the heart
rumbling
like a raincloud
cloaking the eyes again and again

and this whole desert — memory.

*Translated by Gagan Gill and Arlene Zide*

### *Dream*

He'd steal
every one of my dreams

so I could sleep
soundly.

When I woke, he had returned
all my dreams
one by one —

It was
the lure of

rock-bottom.

*Translated by Gagan Gill and Arlene Zide*

### *Everything is a Journey*

Everything is a journey
under his feet
above his head
as if he's walking on a single circuit of the world.

Still, how different
the sensation of his touch
and of his being

on Earth and in the sky
How different
his touch
within me.

*Translated by Gagan Gill and Arlene Zide*

## *Except One Time*

It is somewhere here
just a few steps
and I can see it
One more step
and I can touch it

It is here, somewhere
my whole universe
my whole loneliness
till today

It goes on
Nothing stops
inside it
except for one time

*Translated by Gagan Gill and Arlene Zide*

## *Post-Partum*

Weaving the basket
I didn't know
what I would keep in it
a flower or a dream
or a child
who he would give me
in answer to time's prayer.

Weaving the basket
I didn't know

it was my own blood
I was weaving.

*Translated by Gagan Gill and Arlene Zide*

## *The Difference*

Since I could not forgive
all of them
are alive in my memory

and they think
they're really alive
in my memory.

*Translated by Gagan Gill and Arlene Zide*

## *That Same Incident*

It was a woman's heart
speaking
went on speaking
for eons.

It was a woman's heart
that was quiet
quiet for
centuries

And between them was a mountain
a man or
a mouse
that was gnawing away
even in the amicable moments
at a voice crying out
at a tongue which was numb
right from day one.

*Translated by Gagan Gill and Arlene Zide*

## *The Shadow of the Last Forest*

Memory now is not
just
a fragrance

Every moment
something new adds to it.
some gratitude
some scene cracking apart
some pain.

Sometimes everything was lost in it
Sometimes everything was found.
Sometimes a storm
a river
or a peaceful pervasiveness
of an unarrived love.

Memory is not
just a fragrance
Slinking
within
is the shadow
of the last forest.

*Translated by Gagan Gill and Arlene Zide*

## *Untitled*

Let this last boat
be sunk
The boat
beautiful as a fairy tale

As long as I am in it
wielding this oar
made of the stems of desire
it will neither sink
nor take me across.

Swaying it will go on
in this midstream   in
the middle of the waters of the deep
but I need to cut across it
walking on water
as if water were my own being.

This shore and
that shore too

Perhaps these oars will be
feathers some day
Feathers of water

And will set me down
in the great void

of white waters

On the impossible
next page

of my destiny.

*Translated by Gagan Gill and Arlene Zide*

# KANNADA

## PRATHIBHA NANDAKUMAR

### *For AKR – 1*

I was all that and suddenly

She appeared in the backyard,
where he spoke his mother's tongue.

'Who are you?' I asked

'I am his,' she said,
sitting cross-legged
on the grass mat.

Was she the one he mentioned,
the one who does not wash between her legs?

Perhaps her pan-chewed red lips will now
start speaking the unutterable obscenities.

Was she the one who turned her back to him,
peeling off her clothes, waiting for him
to undo her bra, making him sweat and shudder?

Was she the one
who watched sparrows on the park bench,
like him, not knowing what to say?

Or, wait a minute, the one he took,
shaking a little, as commandments crumbled
behind the laws of his land?

Or the one they found dead
sitting on the toilet seat, naked, in the room
whose numbers vanished to appear again in his poems?

Or the one for whom he waited,
as always, to arrive from
somewhere and take him somewhere?

I watch her breasts to detect signs
of poison smeared, to offer him,
to suck her dry, to renew his breath.

But had she killed him,
the mother turned demon,
or had she kissed away his pain,
as she always did?

In a rage, I slapped her

And she disappeared
into his absent presence.

*Translated by the poet*

## *For AKR – 2*

*Think how many states of being, how many emotions*
*you go through in the course of a single day. Who are you?*
– A.K. Ramanujan

'When will I see you again? '

Stepping into the elevator I ask
as he releases his ushering hand
to shut the door. I ask again, anxious,
turning away to hide my tears
and not face his.

'When are you coming again? '

He is working on Meera's devotion
after going through Akka Mahadevi.
Andal was his favourite last year
Lalla he has heard just now
and Radha never wrote poems.

Returning to the land of
Stars and Stripes,
from the land of black soil,
this elevator closes to
become the no man's land
and I ask him once again

'When again?'

Descending at breakneck speed
running through lifetimes
ages crumbling into a heap
he looks tired, yet happy
with his elusive multiple being

And laughs like Shiva, Krishna
and the Lord of the Blooming Jasmine
all in one and plants that one last kiss
just before the door opens

To take him away and

We stand there comforting each other
Meera, Akka, Andal, Lalla, Radha.

*Translated by the poet*

## *For AKR – 3*

You, who you say, have no proper sense of body,
do not wonder if I wondered too
whether the pulse you stumbled on was yours or mine
You are no fool
In a single day you touched many
in passing, who let you pass
and knew it is never too late for
sin or even treason.
You know my kind.
You have given me
a houseful of legitimate sons
in the course of a single day.
You speak of a look,
my love, look — your angry hands
are speaking many emotions that
prove your many states of being
each knowing exactly who he is.

I belong to all of you.

*Translated by the poet*

## *Honour Killing*

*(A Hindu boy and a Muslim girl eloped, got married and went into hiding. Their families hunted them down and killed them both in front of their one year-old child. No one wanted the child and the police took her into their custody.)*

1

They had covered only half the distance
the mosque was on top of the hill
and the temple on the other side of the cliff

The story ended even before it started.

What do you tell the little one?
That, once upon a time
a foolish man and the queen of scents
were butchered for giving birth to her?

Do not dare peep into the little one's eyes
You cannot answer the questions in them.
Leave it to the *National Geographic*
to capture the blue-green light in them.

God incarnates and sometimes
takes the form of knives and swords.

2

If honour killing is sacred then
we are a very religious country.

If you say you have the answer and
ask what is the question,
you will be hanged.

The blood dries to make black stains
on the roads where once
we played hop-scotch

You can live here only if you are dead.

I am appalled
there is still love in my poems.

3

The scared Brahmin who stepped on the dirt
died of shock. Ganesh festival
can also trigger a communal riot.

I apologised to the dung-bug
sorry, we are only human.
It just continued to roll the dung.

Your best friend is standing behind you
with a gun in hand ready to pull the trigger.

The newspapers carry the story
of a displaced tribe caught stealing in the metro.

*Translated by the poet*

## *Salvation*

*Remembering can be the means to salvation*

– A.K. Ramanujan

1

SALAD DAYS

Oh, they were tender, green, leafy and raw.
Fresh cut, as the breaking-in of a colt
Wild, as the first flight of a nameless bird
floating about the narrow dark alleys
searching for a parking spot to
land and indulge in some peeling, slicing and
sucking of juices with matching exclamations.
Everything got soaked and sprouted.
Those were the days of talking and taking.

2

FASTING DAYS

Everything resembled a dish
Denial was the mantra.
Do not, the anthem.
Pangs hit the diaphragm.
Aching heart, intestines and mouth drying,
To chew was a curse, to swallow a punishment.

Hungry forever, thirsty every minute,
Vastness taking over dilated pupils
To fast was to preserve.
To consume was to serve.
We were on a diet and we meant to quiet
the heart, the intestine, lungs, legs and
the unmentionables, in anticipation of
the next feast.

3

DESSERT DAYS

And then, there was pudding
of all sorts.
Cream, cakes, nuts, fruits,
Exotic ethnic sweets
It was time to indulge.
How many poems make a day?
How many dreams make an hour?
How does the metaphor bird build nests on railings?
Who needs to sanction these constructions?
Those were the days of extravagance and
A phone call away, a filling pizza.

4

SALVATION

And it happened one day.
It was getting crowded.
His elusive multiple beings engulfed
in that one single second, he,

lord of the blue waters,
lost his every appetite and left.
The Jain monks call it *sallekhan.*

If to remember is to find salvation
To forget is to be cursed to return to life.

*Translated by the poet*

## *Not chaste at all*

If it were really a spiritual deal
I would have made a pot out of dry sand
and filled it with water like the Mahasati, Renuka
and scraped dirt off my thighs like Parvathi and made
a Ganesha to stand on guard while I went bathing
like a chaste woman.

Oh, they scare you like hell with stories of women who
were sent to hell or died a tragic death eaten by ants or
punished by the god of virtue for breaking the rule—
the chaste does not desire a man other than her husband.

They have any number of instances to guide you
Like Savitri who won over death just by her words
Or Shakku who carried her sick husband in a basket
to his paramour and waited for him to finish.
Have you ever wondered why it's always only the
Chaste who are chased by lusty ruffians?

Listening to all that, day in and day out, one gets very
grubby and I came here to bathe in this clear water
to wash away the sweat, lathering myself in scented
soaps like in the ads and cleansing my senses
Called out 'oh come on, you, one and all,
Come find your nirvana in my valleys and curves.'

The gods went crazy. Couldn't turn me to stone or
curse me to become a flesh-eating worm.
They couldn't even stop my pen writing
divine songs in perfect meter and rhyme.

And the death penalty?
Well, let's face it when we get to it. Ha.

*Translated by the poet*

## *Between Yes and No*

Why is it that a yes
is a simple yes
and a no is a lifetime of
self-denial, doubt, regret
and a thesis unto itself?

*Translated by the poet*

## *The Yoni Chakra*

The three inverted triangles of the yoni chakra
cut across the four moving upwards
fourteen lotus petals spread around and
nothing goes out of symmetry or colour

As the lines are drawn
fingers tremble and the
central point takes over
it's the expectation of the mating now
that churns a storm in the lower pool

and when the churning begins
what precious things emerge
the fish reach the core of the sanctum
sanctorum and the resulting Tantric designs
with ten thousand eyes suddenly
reveal the squares, crosslines and

there you can see the hitherto hidden
crystal clear
two-petal bud
opening into
a full-fledged flower

and you fulfil the purpose of your birth.

*Translated by the poet*

## *Jogathi*

I walked out, leaving behind
the broken bangles
empty bindi and kohl box
comb with fallen teeth

Pleats hindering brisk steps
peacock in the pallu cackling
fragrant jasmine in the hair
teardrop trembling on the edge of an eyelash
running down the smooth cheek
the cracking sound of leather footwear
here goes the fluttering bird of the cage

On the old familiar well
flipped aside
the tight hugging embroidered blouse
a tear in the drape, caught in the
shoulder ornament
the checkered scarf
with the intoxicating sweat-scent
of the wet body

The dice-playing mother
under a pearl-lined umbrella
called out to come, drink a glass of cool milk.
After choking on it I stepped out,
leaving behind the

lullaby, the cradle
the silver feeding spoon

Unmindful of what I was leaving behind
searched for something else.
Roaming nomadic covering the distances
going in and out through the
moonlight and scorching sun.

Finally standing atop the steep cliff
answering the last final call
Jogathi, wearing the
solitary flower and a lone stud,
consumed by the poison
dances the death dance
and from her neck
there tumbles
the rudraksh.

*Translated by the poet*

## MAMTA G. SAGAR

### *Mother and Me*

I'm exactly like my mother
—thin body, bony fingers,
dark circles below the eyes
within, a heavy heart
loaded with cares; a mind
beset with thoughts it can't
quite carry; and on the surface,
a smooth smile.

I'm exactly like my mother
her tears flow in my eyes.

*Translated by the poet*

### *A River Poem*

Inside the river are
the sky, the cloud and the sun.
Cupped in my hands is the river.

If I throw up my hands
the river spills, scattering
sky, cloud and sun all over me.

If I drink the river from my hands

then within me are
the sun, the clouds, the sky.

Tell me then, who is in whom?

*Translated by the poet*

## *Claustrophobic*

A square —
the kitchen, the hall, the bedroom
neat squares.
The mattress, the cot, the bedsheet
perfect squares.

The book, the table, the chair
. . . the stream of thought
everything is within
this square barrier.

The door, the roof, the wall
white tiles laid on the floor
finally,
the fragment of sky
the ventilator admits in
— all have corners four.

The roundness of the earth stands suspect.
If words jump out

if they leave the page, if
they escape the meaning-barrier,
then, soundless forms
unbound limits.

Here, sense of space
changes to its converse
— space stretches endless . . .

so much of space
lies within S P A C E

*Translated by Chitra Panikkar*

## *Talking About Dharma/Adharma**

*Hara hara mahadeva!*
shouts from throats filled with poison
rends these bodies

poison in the throat
seeps into the vein,
poison of the mind
renders the body blue

spreads blue poison across the sky
turns the corals and pearls in the ocean's depth blue
this is the time

the cradle of death swings with a lullaby
laa . . . laa . . . la lullaby

child, take care —
the butcher's knife glistens
in the pool of flesh and blood
just two inches below the navel
sharpness slits through
even before the scream is out
manliness is proved and achieved

The breast, the vagina,
breast-milk, the monthly
flow of blood — all have
different meanings
in the politics of dharma

here, hands, feet, head, torso,
love, affection, sorrow
are all soaked in blood

a wink of sleep for the pain
a tear or two for the hated
a little compassion in the heart
that is *dharma.*

*Translated by Chitra Panikkar and the poet*

* The year 2002 saw the worst communal clashes in modern Indian history, triggered by Hindu fundamentalists/political organisations in Gujarat. This poem was a response to that violence.

## VAIDEHI

### *Don't Look into the Vanity Bag*

It's not right to slip your hands
into the vanity bag and look, oh men,
Vanity can contain much
Should one reveal it all?

Mirror, comb, kajal box
Pen, powder, clip, perfume
white paper, a spool of thread,
buttons, a needle, a supari
a few tamarind seeds, too!
And need one find only
channa in the bag?
There could be a mint and *Comfit* as well.

You may find dried leaves and flowers,
a route map to someone's house,
The cool comfort of red-oxide floor
under a wooden slab
infinite memories,
bindi sticker, a leaf, fragrance,
a peacock feather that could spawn
a smaller one,
the treasures of childhood,
sand, mud from who knows where?

A half-written poem, hovering perhaps
in the dark depths
a hanky holding a sigh that was
trapped in the throat
an addressed envelope
containing only a picture of the red sun
a letter received — breathing a riddle,
meaningless doodles surrounding
writing in a beautiful hand
an ecstatic tune,
a nameless photo with a
black moustache and a flashy smile.

A pouch containing
shadows of childhood, youth, old age.
Different personae of a married woman,
lover and adulteress
merging into one
under dharma and the prescribed norms.
Don't odd pairs come together
for no reason at all?
So do the worlds in the bag!

Do you think the worlds of vanity and
emotion are the same?
Foolish men,
don't exercise your minds.
This equation is beyond you.

You can never look into the mind
All is hidden.
And if, somehow, you do get to peep in,
You will still not find the truth of the vanity bag.
And even if you do
Never, never look into a vanity bag.

*Translated by Prathibha Nandakumar*

## *She, He and Language*

'I am hungry, thirsty,' she said.
'Have a good meal, have a drink,' he said.
Then she started crying.
He laughed.

The other day, he talked about the window
and not the door as she thought.
When he mentioned the wall
she thought he was talking about the open space —
Was it because everything is open
when a wall is broken?

She made payasam, she knew he would like it,
He ate it thinking it was rayatham.

Why is everything so topsy-turvy?

Was there no wind blowing

from one to the other
and so no waves?
Heads down, words in water
send out a forlorn cry.

It was then that suicide was mentioned.
What did he say?
He found it funny, didn't he?

That is the way it is sometimes, you see.
A thing turns out to be something else —
The sea isn't a sea
And what we thought was the shore
is only the backs of fish.

'Be honest and tell me,
which one of us is more insane?' she asked.
He asked in return,
'Is it the one who wants to die first?'

'It's so hot. Shall I open the window so that
the wind blows between us?' she said.

'What did you say?' he asked
Did you say you are hungry and thirsty?'

*Translated by Ramachandra Sharma*

*Payasam:* a sweet dish, generally prepared on happy and festive occasions, while *rayatham* with buttermilk in it is anything but sweet.

## *Tell Me, You Who Know . . .*

Tell me,
You who know poetry,
I know nothing of it.
But I know what rasam is.

Do you think that's nothing?
Rasam calls for a blend
of the principles of water,
aroma and essence —
a tempered state reached after simmering . . .

Thus . . .

There it was in the corner
a container with rasam
on a seemingly dead and ash-covered
coal fire, waiting . . .
Does it matter that it waits?

In the great durbar of meat dishes
seasoned with spices that sparkled,
Of servers who danced as they walked,
Of laughter and chatter,
It had waited since morning
the clear rasam on a seemingly dead
coal fire, simmering,
still fresh, even at night.

You who know all about poetry,
tell me,
Do you know what rasam is?
Forgive me,
I don’t know any poetry.

*Translated by Ramachandra Sharma*

# SA USHA

## *To My Mother*

Mother, don't, please don't
Don't cut off the sunlight
With your sari spread across the sky
Blanching life's green leaves

Don't say: you're seventeen already
Don't flash your sari in the street
Don't make eyes at passers-by
Don't be a tomboy riding the wind

Don't play that tune again
That your mother,
Her mother and her mother
Had played on the snake-charmer's flute
Into the ears of nitwits like me

I am just spreading my hood
I'll sink my fangs into someone
And leave my venom
Let go, make way

Circumambulating the holy plant
In the yard, making rangoli designs
To see heaven, turning up dead

Without light and air.
For God's sake, I can't do it.

Breaking out of the dam
You've built, swelling
In a thunderstorm
Roaring through the land,
Let me live very differently
From you, mother.

Let go, make way.

*Translated by A.K. Ramanujan*

# BENGALI

## NABANEETA DEV SEN

### *The Jungle Story*

my exile is over, mother,
no more living in the jungle for me
come, mother, underneath this matted beard
feel the familiar cheeks of your child
open up your breasts, mother, and see how
the seven streams of milk
gush towards my parched tongue

look at these feet, mother, the tiny feet
where your golden bells had jingled
look at this arm
upon which you had tied your talisman
when I was born
now look at this chest where you had planted
the sapling of a heart
in a soft green stretch of sun
in the hidden mesh of this dark jungle,
impenetrable,
has grown a hungry tree . . .
with toothy leaves and sharp claws
and fierce flowers
it chews on other hearts
a fine flesh-eater

my time in the jungle is over, mother,
now the jungle lives in me.

*Translated by the poet and* tlm

## *Fourteen*

fourteen sticks to my hair like a blob of chewing gum
adolescence in my palms
moonwax trickling over my brow
sum total: zero
dream upon dream
sum total: zero
like adding dew to the wind . . .
this green mantle
inside my eyes   filling my eyes   covering my eyes
spread out on the dust
this green mantle
step on it for a moment

should I call it love
should I call it longing
inside my head these dark forests
in my heart these sixty miles of empty highway
desolate
jamming my jaws, rocks
choking my throat, sand dunes
roaring inside my head, cascades
within my eyes   filling my eyes   overflowing my eyes

the moon
stars at my fingertips
adolescence in my palms
five rivers gushing out between the fingers of my clenched
fist
the tears of the teens melt into the air
unfree.

*Translated by the poet and* tlm

## *Return of the Dead*

Receive me then, Calcutta,
I am your first love,
Your childhood sweetheart
Hear I am, an aborted mother
I have brought the ocean with me instead
My arms are empty, yes, but my breasts
Are heavy, overflowing with wasted milk
Look at the fathomless salt water

Come, look at me, then,
Virginity glows on my brow again
Naked as the setting sun
Touch me, Calcutta, my newborn flesh
Belongs to you now
Receive me in your waiting arms
Your loneliness is over
Your prayers were heard

I have returned, just as you
Would have liked me to

Why this stunned silence, then?
Lift up your chin
Don't shift your eyes
Speak to me
Here she is, returned from the dead
As you had wished
Look at me — yes, I am she,
Your old flame, your world of passion
Your very own
Nabaneeta.

*Translated by the poet*

## *These Fond Faces like Clouds*

I cannot bear to watch
My people become old

With naked eyes I cannot bear to see
These familiar faces dissolve like clouds.
Around the pools of the eyes, pond scum gathers
Brows drawn up like a dead bird's wings
Lie flat on their faces
Lips dry up like raw fruit torn by storms
Drying in the dust
How everything dries

How everything flies away with the wind
Paper shreds, everything

The heart folds up its tent and steps out into the road
Ready to raise its hand and stop any streetcar
To raise its hand in farewell and leave
How the heart folds up
How the heart sweeps off the gleaming pots and pans
From the rack onto the stone floor
With a terrible crash
How all sounds lose themselves in the heat
All signs dissolve
All bridges break
These fond faces change their shape like clouds
And float away

With naked eyes I cannot bear to see
The scorched grass in my courtyard
So very near.

*Translated by the poet*

## *Dharavi, 1992*

dishes are being shattered
small utensils
that make a poor man's household

dishes are being shattered

with a deafening noise
like the demolition of a rich man's mansion
shaking up the neighbours' walls

only glasses are breaking

only glasses are breaking
what's so surprising about it?
what's surprising is
this quaking earth
this bubbling blood
this breathless sky
this demented air

only a poor man's household is being shattered
what's so poor about it?
in a poor man's home
poverty has no name
it melts away
like pain
water to water
air to air

in spite of it
lo and behold
a poor man's household is being shattered
with a terrible crash
air is piercing air
water floats on water

do you hear the roaring soil?
the rumbling thunder
that hissing rising from the deep?
Sorrow, the foundation serpent
Is pouring out its poison
On earth's thirty-two umbilical cords

In the womb of a drunken mother
Form the flames of hell
Every hull of rice
Fills with a kernel of volcanic ash
Every blade of grass
Turns into a spear
In the hand
Of a sibling

*Translated by the poet*

## *I Give to Baser Life*

I have no need for earth or water
Just fire, air and space
Wipe out the breasts, the waist, the luring eyes
Wipe out tears and laughter
Take back your earth and water

I'll keep my skies.

*Translated by the poet*

## *A Birthday Voodoo*

*On Ruth Feldman's 85th Birthday, 1996*

I am reading your poems, Ruth,
 and thinking of relationships
between speechless animals and grains of rice
also speechless
between stars and planets
between the sea and water
between us

I am thinking about relationships
 between yesterdays and tomorrows
The magical relationship
between space and time

Can't blame poor memory cells
How much can they bear
How much can they wipe out
Witness Cheat Witness Cheat Witness

The magic of time
sometimes works only in one direction
like turning black into grey
but sometimes it also flows against the current
and shatters the unshatterable
that is the Voodoo of time

otherwise in this warm afternoon

in the sweltering heat of Calcutta
reading your poems about the snow-drizzling Boston sky
why should I think of time
tail in mouth  mouth in tail
unbroken   unbreakable

I can see you, Ruth, at your computer
Playing with Primo,your old friend,
Those burning ovens,
Those beautiful lampshades made of fine skin,
Those fashion wigs of human hair,
I can smell the fumes
And I see it all turning  gently, ever so gently, into English
As the hidden children
Grow up into over-exposed adults

From a faraway corner of this planet, the same one,
I am watching it all, Ruth,
I am watching it all as I run
The running away never ends . . .

Happy Birthday, Ruth, Woman of the Riverbank,
I give you this glass window
And the open balcony
With the saffron river next to it, and all the boats
With their naked white sails and naked black sailors rowing
I give you the steamer's midnight whistle on the Ganga
The very same that you heard as a young girl on the
    Mississippi

I give you this old, old banyan tree by the river
looking like a Rastafarian with
all its roots hanging from the branches like dreadlocks,
I give you the strong wind and the strong current, let it all
flow through your joined hands

Happy Birthday, Ruth, I can see you
With your easel and your paintbrushes,
Against the red-gold autumn sky . . .
keep the empowering memories
and the dreams that follow
Keep Algiers and Siracusa,
keep the Himalayas and the Taj Mahal

I want to wrench from you
Buchenwald

*Translated by the poet*

## DEBARATI MITRA

### *Train Time*

At dawn   quarter to five   the train like Dodo's skeleton
At morning   nine   a bird, thick rice-fields.
When it's eleven-thirty
Accumulated rain-water in a soft sand-hole.
Afternoon   quarter to three
Three or four moths companionless all day.

Evening   six forty-three
Warm aroma and flavour of roasted chicken
At nine thirty-four   almost cruelty
Loving bee-sting.
At night   one fifty-five
Darkness like Kali's womb, alone.

*Translated by Sanjukta Dasgupta*

### *Applied Mathematics*

Two and two make four
I can't believe this any longer.
Mixing two and two can breed a piglet
Or perhaps the Manhattan project for atomic bombs.
There the sun is like a fish that escapes tearing the line
And disappears into the depths of the river
And that boy gathering cabbage

Following the horizon line in a parallel shadow
The trundling train advances
All signifying evening
But there's no connection between them.

A couple, a man and woman, chatting for 45 minutes
Husband-wife, or ordinary lovers
They just can't be.
Not brother-sister, nor keya blossoms - sravan month
What then?
I don't want to calculate the wind
Nor the watch.

If the colour blue is added to the bird's flight path
Would the result be sky?
If a long sigh is added to the mirror's reflection
Would it be I?
All caterpillars + two wings
Aren't butterflies.

Having observed all these
I flung my newly composed book of applied mathematics
into the sky.
A senior star
Flipping through the pages fluttered its eyes
Said : Atheist.

*Translated by Sanjukta Dasgupta*

## *Kiki*

Who, why, when, no one knows.
On the seashore   waist deep in sand
Was found the girl, Kiki of Jade House
In the far north near the waterline
Long hair and lapping waves
Have covered her body partly,
The salty caress of the sea has washed away her streaming
    blood.

Black bruise like fish bile on her throat
A bit of tongue sticks out like
A cuckoo's deformed voice
On her thighs not men's caresses
But faint sores from cigarette burns
Yet her lidless, shark-nibbled eyes
Still dream.

Feet on a bed of sand
The sea pillows her head
Rippling brains sing along with the waves
Everything's almost all right.

Only in secret tonight
Not roasted chicken
Kiki's little finger
Was served in silverware
On her stepfather's dining table.

*Translated by Sanjukta Dasgupta*

## MITHU SEN

### *Bahia*

dead fish on the beach
becoming earth
sand —
no longer a fish —
becoming a pattern

~

I lift my skirt
to walk the sea

~

I kiss your mouth —
you translate my tongue

~

It reeks everywhere —
the smell of caneleira
of cinnamon tree —

in my tea
in your breath

~

I'll see you soon
in my next life —

if you are late —
I will walk

~

gradually
the waters close —
nothing to grasp
nothing to flow

~

I am —
yes I am
becoming
someone else —
for a while

~

I think of the time
we decorated our house
with plants and waters

~

hold my wrists —

I don't want to listen
to that old fortune-teller
any more — never

~

it is so dark —
not even the face
of whom I love
can be seen

~

I could not go to you

because I was
the other woman

~

song to be sung —
under the tree
under the sea
under me

that crime
I haven't committed yet —

but longing for
the same river
river bed

intricate paths
vessels
the same veins    wrinkles
the same you
balanced    unbalanced

no light, no dark
no shade, instead
so flat — damn flat

send me some shadows
send me some greys —
let me feel the dimensions

I laughed
until
there were tears
in our eyes

I make paper boats
send them to friends —
'burn them' I request
some did, some did not

~

I found
a chain with a pendant —
this is 'good luck'
in Bahia

I found two 'good lucks'
on the beach
last evening

~

with the tidal flow —
let me be boiled alive

~

no exit
let myself be nailed

no exit
let myself be nailed

~

no schedule
no agenda
no 'shoulds' —

an uncharted time
I am restless —
~
shifted and shifted —
deleted
and edited —
~

*Transcreated by Sudeep Sen*

## *Magpie, Sparrow*

In my home's many rooms — sparrows, magpies nest.
I weep on their wings — they too weep embracing me.
Eye's lashes embrace tears — tear's lashes embrace eyes.
In my home's many rooms — sparrows, magpies nest.

If sadness is bird's wings — if sadness is wind's flight,
real sadness is mourning. Is real sadness dying?
That death is ice-still eyes — eyes' tears enclosing ash.
In my heart-chamber's many rooms — sparrows, magpies
nest.

*Translated by Sudeep Sen*

### *'You lie down — in your lone, bleak room'*

You lie down — in your lone, bleak room.
I, too, lie — speechless, feverish.
Let our distance now — be immortal.

*Translated by Sudeep Sen*

### *'What you touched — I did not'*

What you touched — I did not.
May I touch you — if only, just?

*Translated by Sudeep Sen*

### *'Moment I stepped on two boats'*

Moment I stepped on two boats —
Both feet turned into stones.

*Translated by Sudeep Sen*

### *'On your hand — I place my hand — barely'*

On your hand — I place my hand — barely.
          In our hands — nothing.

*Translated by Sudeep Sen*

## MANDAKRANTA SEN

### *The Witch*

One who writes poetry in the middle of the night
With her hair undone is a witch.

After everyone's asleep, she soaks in clear moonlight
On netherworld's roof — she doesn't know which.

Secretly she roasts, then eats the pulpy sadness
Plucked from the crown of her head.

Climbs up her throat — no lyric of love and caress,
Rather an acidic belch-like moon instead.

As soon as it is dawn she conceives the sun
Getting to full-blown advanced stage by noon.

Bathing with her young dad, she beats the water in fun —
A young woman struck by the moon.

*Translated by Sudeep Sen and the poet*

## *Full Moon: An Untimely One*

Ever since that afternoon,
Even the pale moon looked lost in a trance.

She who had stopped bleeding
From the eighth day of the past dark fortnight

At the corner of her mouth, traces of drug
Or poison, can still be found.

What made her think that inside her bloodstream
She could still take such a chance?

With a faint retching sound, the entire roof was
Flooded with vomit, moonlight

Warm milk filled her ancient breasts that
Aren't that round any more.

*Translated by Sudeep Sen and the poet*

## *An Aphorism for Death*

O joy personified — I bow before you and pray.
Today is so auspicious — it is the goat sacrifice day.

From the bloodline of elixir that goat was bred
Glue-nectar holds together its torso and head.

Ambrosia he eats and nectar he drinks
Death is his elixir — can't you see the link?

Because it's death alone who can consume the potion
Potatoes are served to you, obeying old notion.

O joy personified — you relish slaughter like spice
That's why you're served a spicy dish of frustrated rice.

It's slaughter that is your food and your drink as well
How do you digest them? — Come on, please tell.

So that I check my puke at the sacrificial block
O executioner, I bow before you. You rock.

*Translated by Sudeep Sen and the poet*

## *A Letter from Lesbos*

Blood on her face, chest; blood between her legs —
This wild smell of blood has made me crave and beg.

This fleshy smell of blood has made me lust for more —
In the sea of desire, *this* is the triangular shore.

Is she a man, or a woman? — Who's there to determine?
I've seen her in the dark — she is my light, she's mine.

*Translated by Sudeep Sen and the poet*

## *Nature Goddess*

Packing my groin, my navel, my buttocks in a sack
I left my home for the sloping wrong side of the track.

The male flower in my yard has the usual calyx and pollen,
But it is by Nature Goddess that my heart is stolen.

Here is a plantation of lies — a land of hate, fear and shame.
And there is a ravine, lying on her back, like lust untamed.

Lust is very clever; she knows my story well —
Where I am heading to land in coveted hell.

Don't care who doesn't know — I'll tell the wind and sky
Domestic life is poison to me, without Nature I will die.

Yes, not a man, with *you* I'll start a fresh trek
Along the peaks of your breasts — and a vagina like a
mountain lake.

*Translated by Sudeep Sen and the poet*

## *Left & Right*

Don't want to call. Still — please wait a bit.
Worship hall to your right, to the left the red-light street.

Which one do you desire? Think man, think real hard —
Here are two worlds smeared with menstrual blood.

Don't want to leave you. But that's the inevitable course.
Altar of Goddess to the right, to the left a colony of whores.

Where do you desire to go? Think man, think, and tell
me —
Where would you find your blood-smeared happiness key?

Don't want to tell you. Yet for truth's sake just let me tell —
You've got heaven on your right, on your left you've got hell.

You think you can manage both sides? Very smart.
I *am* your Goddess, man, believe me — I *am* your tart.

*Translated by Sudeep Sen and the poet*

*Agreement*

Everything else apart from this, everything you love to
fiddle —
These breasts, this belly with a slit-wound right in the middle
Where germs have dug more intricate bends and turns,
You may take all its pus and blood. The pain is what I've
earned.

There is much more — the navel taken off in the middle of
the night;
The nipples, the pubic hair, the armpits where you planted
your rights;
The skin where your teeth and tongue embossed a blood-red
seal —
Please tally the balance, see how each stanza fits the bill.

Check it out whether there are any flaws left somewhere;
Call on witnesses if you want, I will strip naked I swear.
I wouldn't hide even the smallest naevus from your lust,
You'll get everything you wish. But the rest that's lying on
dust —

Picking that clean from my own body, mind and soul
Fiercely I guard.
You can never ever have me as a whole.

*Translated by Sudeep Sen and the poet*

# PREVIOUS PUBLICATION

**Meena Alexander**

'Rites of Sense', 'Torn Grass' and 'Pale Blouses', From *Quickly Changing River* (TriQuarterly Books/ Northwestern University Press, 2008).

'South of the Nilgiris', from *River and Bridge* (Rupa, 1995).

'Amrita' from *Raw Silk* (TriQuarterly Books/ Northwestern University Press, 2004).

**Anamika**

'Unemployed', 'Unanswerable Questions' and 'Salt', from *Aria* (Yeti Books and Mulfran Press, 2010)

**Temsula Ao**

'Nowhere Boatman', 'Trophies', 'Man to Woman', 'Woman to Man' and 'The Leaf Shredder', from *Songs from the Other Life: Poems* (Grasswork Books, 2007).

**Sampurna Chattarji**

'Mother and Daughter: A Duet', 'Fairytale', 'Object Lesson: Three' and 'Object Lesson: Seven', from *Sight May Strike You Blind* (Sahitya Akademi, 2007; 2008).

'Where do I put this Love', from *Indian Literature*, 243 (Jan-Feb 2008).

'Let No One', from the unpublished collection *Absent Muses.*

**Mamang Dai**

'Voice of the Mountain', from *We Speak in Changing Languages: Indian Women Poets 1990-2007* (Sahitya Akademi, 2009).

'The Sorrow of Women' and 'Incalculable Days', from *Dancing Earth: An Anthology of Poetry from North-East India* (Penguin, 2009).

**Kamala Das**

'Composition', 'Blood', 'Glass', 'Convicts', 'An Introduction', 'My Grandmother's House' and 'The Stone Age', from *The Old Playhouse and Other Poems* (Orient Longman, 1973).

**Gauri Deshpande**

'The Habit', from *Between Births* (Writer's Workshop, 1968).

'Prometheus and Orpheus', 'Between Births' and 'Poems on a Lost Love', from *Lost Love* (Writer's Workshop, 1970).

'Workaday Women' and 'The Female of the Species', from *Beyond the Slaughterhouse* (Dialogue Publications, 1972).

**Amita Kokate**

'One Should Take', from *Live Update: An Anthology of Recent Marathi Poetry* (Poetrywala, 2005).

**Kavita Mahajan**

'Depraved', 'Modest' and 'A Doubt', from *Live Update: An Anthology of Recent Marathi Poetry* (Poetrywala, 2005).

**Jyotsna Milan**

'A Little Bit More', 'As If Never', and 'Search' from *Anthology of Hindi Women Poets* (Sahitya Akademi, forthcoming).

**Rukmini Bhaya Nair**

'Gulmohur', from *We Speak in Changing Languages: Indian Women Poets 1990-2007* (Sahitya Akademi, 2009).

**Mandakranta Sen**

'The Witch', 'Full Moon: An Untimely One', 'An Aphorism for Death', 'A Letter from Lesbos', 'Nature Goddess', 'Left & Right' and 'Agreement', from *Aria* (Yeti Books and Mulfran Press, 2010).

**Mithu Sen**

'Doel, Sparrow', 'You lie down —in your lone bleak room', 'What you touched — I did not', 'Moment I stepped on two boats', 'On your hand- I place my hand- barely' and 'Bahia', from *Aria* (Yeti Books and Mulfran Press, 2010).

**Nabaneeta Dev Sen**

'The Jungle Story' and 'Fourteen', from *the little magazine*, vol. 1, issue 1.

**Rajee Seth**

'Fear', 'It Can't Ever See, the Sky' and 'Mughal Garden', from *Anthology of Hindi Women Poets* (Sahitya Akademi, forthcoming).

**Malika Amar Sheikh**

'A Poem for a Dali Painting', 'Metropolis' and 'Venus', from *Live*

*Update: An Anthology of Recent Marathi Poetry* (Poetrywala, 2005).

**Menka Shivdasani**

'Spring-Cleaning', 'Why Rabbits Never Sleep', 'The Quality of Darkness', 'Epitaph', 'The Secret Pool', 'Kitchen Dreams', 'A World Within' and 'Marionette', from *Stet* (myword! PRESS, 2003).

**Archana Varma**

'Man', 'Protection' and 'Watch' from *Anthology of Hindi Women Poets* (Sahitya Akademi, forthcoming).

# POETS

**Meena Alexander** is Distinguished Professor of English at the City University of New York. Her work in poetics includes a book of poems and essays, *The Shock of Arrival: Reflections on Postcolonial Experience.* Among her volumes of poetry are *Stone Roots; House of a Thousand Doors; River and Bridge; Illiterate Heart* (winner of the PEN Open Book Award); *Raw Silk;* and two chapbooks, each a single long poem. Her new anthology, *Quickly Changing River,* appeared in February 2008.

**Anamika** teaches English literature at Satyawati College, Delhi University and has published on feminist poetics, contemporary poetry and gender issues. Her collections of poetry are *Beejakshar* (1989), *Anushtup* (1995), *Khurduri Hathlliyan* (2005), *Kavita Mein Aurat* (2004), and *Doob-Dhan* (2007).

**Temsula Ao**, poet, scholar and novelist, is currently Dean of the School of Humanities and Education at North Eastern Hill University, Shillong. Awarded the Padma Shri in 2007, she has authored four volumes of poetry: *Laburnum on my Head*; *Songs of Many Moods: A Collection of Poems*; *Songs from the Other Life: Poems* and *Songs from Here and There: A Fourth Collection of Poems.*

**Amrita Bharati** has written seven books of poetry and a volume of prose. Informed by her study of Sanskrit, and an intimate knowledge of Sri Aurobindo's work (she has translated several of his poems into Hindi), her poems contain numerous references to Vedantic ideas, Tantric images and Krishna bhakti. Among her published works are *Harivansh Gatha* (2004); *Sannate Mein Dur Tak*; *Aadmi Ke Aranya Mein*; and *Bhavbhooti* (2000).

**Sampurna Chattarji** is a writer, poet and translator. Her poetry has appeared in anthologies and journals, including *First Proof: The Penguin Book of New Writing from India 2,* and *the little magazine.* Her poetry also features in *Imagining Ourselves: Global Voices from a New Generation of Women,* an anthology commemorating International

Women's Day, 2006. Her first volume of poems, *Sight Can Strike You Blind* was published in 2007; a novel, *Rupture*, appeared in 2009.

**Challapalli Swaroopa Rani** is a Dalit feminist writer teaching at Nagarjuna University, Guntur. Among her publications is a collection of poems, *Mankenapuvvu* (2005), and several short stories and essays published in academic journals and felicitation volumes. She has received the Susheela Narayan Reddy Trust Award (2002), and the Vimala Santhi Sahitya Puraskaram (2006), among others.

**Mamang Dai**, one-time civil servant and currently journalist based in her native Arunachal Pradesh, has published both prose and poetry. *Arunachal Pradesh: The Hidden Land* (2003), received the state's first annual Verrier Elwin prize in publication and print media. Her other work includes *River Poems*; *Mountain Harvest: The Food of Arunachal Pradesh*; and a collection of stories, *The Legends of Pensam.*

**Kamala Das** has published several novels and short stories in English and Malayalam under the pseudonym, Madhavikutty. In English, her work includes the novel, *Alphabet of Lust* (1977); a collection of short stories, *Padmavati the Harlot and Other Stories* (1992); and five books of poetry: *The Old Playhouse and Other Poems* (1973); *The Annamalai Poems* (1985); *Only the Soul Knows how to Sing* (1986); and *Yaa Allah* (2001). She has also published a controversial autobiography, *My Story* (1976). Kamala Das passed away in 2009.

**Sanskritirani Desai**, born in 1958, has degrees in Statistics and Business Administration. The recipient of several prestigious awards, she has published two collections of poems, *Suryoj Suryo* and *Sapnevatemarguo*, and translated poems from Russian and English into Gujarati.

**Gauri Deshpande**, whose work includes poetry, essays and short stories in Marathi and English, has been published extensively in both languages. A translator, one of her most outstanding works was the translation into Marathi of the 16-volume *The Arabian Nights* by Sir Richard Burton. Her collections of poetry include *Between Births* (1968); *Lost Love* (1970); and *Beyond the Slaughterhouse* (1972). Among her prose works are *The Lackadaisical Sweeper* (1997), and the English translation of *Ahe Manohar Tari.*

**Nabaneeta Dev Sen**, poet, novelist, essayist and short story writer is perhaps best loved for her humorous fiction and travel narratives. With more than 50 titles spanning 10 genres, she has broken new ground by repeatedly writing about taboo subjects in Bengali literature—AIDS, drug addiction, trans-sexuality, homosexuality and same-sex love—in a natural, humane way. Among her novels are: *Ami Anupam* (1978); *Swabhumi* (1986); *Maayaa Roye Gelo* (2000); *Albatross* (2004); and, recently, *Ramdhan Mittir Lane* (2006). Her most recent poetry anthology, *Shreshhta Kabita*, appeared in 1989. Among the 25 major awards that she has received are the Padma Shri (2000), the Bharat Nirman Award (2000), the National Sahitya Akademi Award (1999), the Celli Award of the Rockefeller Foundation (1993), Mahadevi Varma Award (1992) and Kavi Puraskar (1976). She has also been honoured as National Poet, All India Radio (1985).

**Saroop Dhruv**, poet and activist, has been involved in anti-communal work in Gujarat since 2002. *Dilma Chhe Ek Ash* (The Heart Remains Hopeful) is the title of the street play that she and Hiren Gandhi staged for Aman Samudaya. Her latest collection of poems is entitled *Hastakshep* (Intervention), an affirmation of a writer's power to intervene. In 2008, she won the Hellman/ Hammett award for courageous writing, given by Human Rights Watch, USA.

**Ghantasala Nirmala** has received several awards for her poetry anthology *Nirvachanam*. They include the Best Book of the Writer (2003) and Sahiti Puraskaram for free verse (2005) from the Potti Sreeramulu Telugu University. She has also received the Free Verse Front Award (2004). She is a journalist and lives in Hyderabad.

**Gagan Gill** has published four collections of poetry: *Ek Din Lautegi Larki* (One Day She Will Return, 1989); *Andhere Mein Buddha* (The Buddha in Darkness, 1996); *Yeh Akanksha Samay Nahin* (This is not the Time of Desire, 1998); and *Thapak Thapak, Dil, Thapak Thapak* (2003); as well as a book of essays, *Dilli mein Uninde* (Sleepless in Delhi, 2000). She has edited a special number of *Yatra* on *New Women Writing in Hindi* (1995), and written a travel account, *Jo Bhi Ishwar ko Dekhta Hai.*

**Bilqees Zefirul Hasan** was born in 1938 into an educated but conservative family. She started writing poetry late in life, and has published two collections of poems, *Geela Eendhan* (Damp Fuel), in 1996, and *Sholon ke Darmiyan* (Amidst the Flames), in 2004. She is also a playwright.

**Ilampirai** is the pen-name of Panchavarnam. She holds a graduation degree in Tamil, and works as a teacher. Her works include *Maunakkuudu* (1993); *Nisaptham* (1998); *Muthal Manusi* (2003); and *Piragoru Naal* (2005). She has received several awards, including the Tamil Nadu government award for her poetry.

**Manisha Joshi** has worked as a print and television journalist in Mumbai and London. Her poetry has appeared in literary magazines like *Indian Literature, New Quest* and *Sandhi,* and has also been published as two collections of poems: *Kandara,* in 1996, and *Kansara Bazaar* in 2001.

**Vasanth Kannabiran** is a feminist poet, translator and founder member of Asmita Resource Centre for Women, Hyderabad. She is co-author of *We Were Making History* (1992); and *De-Eroticizing Assault: Essays on Modesty, Honour and Power* (2002); and co-editor of *Web of Deceit: Devadasi Reform in Colonial India* (2003).

**Kshama Kaul,** poet and writer, portrays the struggle and pain of the Kashmiri woman. Her novel, *Dardpur* (City of Pain, 2004) has been acclaimed as a frank exploration of themes such as exile and communal history.

**Amita Kokate** is a poet and visual artist whose collection of poems, *Canvas,* was published in 1998. She is vice-president of Bharati Astivanga Vikalanga Sanstha, a non-government organisation run by the handicapped for the handicapped, for their rehabilitation.

**Kondepudi Nirmala** was born in 1957, and is an extensively published poet and short story writer, also involved in the broadcast industry as a voice over-artiste. Among her published collections of poetry are *Nadicha Gaayaalu* (Wounds that Walk) and *Sandhigdha Sandhya* (Doubtful Twilight).

**Lalitha Lenin,** poet and social worker, is Reader in the Department of Library and Information Science, University of Kerala. Her collections of poetry include *Karingili* (1976); *Karkidavavu* (1995); *Namukkuprarthikkam* (2000); and *Kadal* (2000). She has also published a novel for children, *Minnu,* and *Puthiya Vaayana,* a book on reading for women.

**Pradnya Lokhande** is among the most acclaimed of today's young Marathi poets. She has been writing for nearly two decades, and most of her work is contained in her three published anthologies, *Antahstha* (1996); *Utkat Jiwaghenya Dhagiwa*; and *Mi Bhidawu Pahatey Samagrashi Dola.*

**Kavita Mahajan**'s collection of poems is entitled *Tatpurush* (2005). She has also edited a book on Warli folk songs, *Warli Lokagite*, and is the author of a novel, *Bra* (mute speech).

**Uma Maheswari** writes both poetry and prose. Her collections of poems include *Natchathirangalin Naduve* (1990); *Verum Pozhuthu* (2002); and *Karpavai* (2004). She has also published two volumes of stories, *Marapaachi* (2002) and *Tholai Kadal* (2004), and received the Katha award for the best short story in Tamil in 2003.

**Malathy Maithri** is a Tamil poet-activist and founder secretary of Ananku, a forum for feminist activities. Her published collections include *Sankarabarani* (2002); *Niirinindri Amalyaathu Ulagu* (2003); and *Niili* (2005). A series of articles, originally published in the magazine *Theranadi*, were compiled and published as *Viduthalai Ezhutthuthal* in 2004.

**Jyotsna Milan** has published two collections of poems: *Ghar Nahin* and *Apne Aagey Aagey*; four books of short stories: *Cheekh ke Aar Paar*; *Khandhar*; *Andhere Mein Intezaar* and *Ummeed ki Doosri Surat;* and two novels: *Apne Saath* and *A Astu Ka.* She has also written about, and translated Gujarati poetry, and been a long-standing editor of the women's journal *Anasuuyaa*, published by the Self-Employed Women's Association (SEWA).

**Debarati Mitra** has published eight collections of poetry. Her resolve to write a poetry that is resolutely 'modern in subject and style' has earned her a distinctive place in Bengali literature. Her first book, *Andha Skoole Ghanta Baje*, was published in 1974. She received the Ananda Puraskar for poetry in 1995.

**Panna Naik** is a librarian/lecturer in Gujarati at the University of Pennsylvania, who has also published five volumes of Gujarati poetry. Her poems have appeared in English translation in several journals, and *In Their Own Voice: The Penguin Anthology of Contemporary Indian Woman Poets.* Her short stories have been widely anthologised, and a collection published in 2003.

**Rukmini Bhaya Nair** is a poet and Professor of Linguistics and English at the Indian Institute of Technology, Delhi. Described by poet Keki Daruwalla as the author of "the first significant volume of post-modern poetry written by an Indian", she has published three volumes of poetry: *The Hyoid Bone* (1992); *The Ayodhya Cantos* (1999); and most recently, *Yellow Hibiscus* (2004).

**Prathibha Nandakumar** is a Bangalore-based poet, short story writer and playwright, and has also been active as a journalist and documentary filmmaker. She has five collections of poetry: *Navu Hudugiyare Heege* (1983); *Itanaka* (1988); *Rasteyanchina Gaadi* (1991); *Kavadeyata* (1998); and *Aha! Purushakaram!* (2000) to her credit. Her two books of short fiction are *Yaana* (1997); and *Akramana* (1997). She has also published translations, essays, and an autobiography.

**Jameela Nishat** writes in Hyderabadi Urdu and seeks to preserve Deccani culture. Two of her anthologies of poetry are *Lava* (2000); and *Lamhe ki Ankh* (2002); she has also edited an anthology, *Inkeshaf* (2000), which features the work of 40 women poets. Among her awards are the Guru Gyanananda Award (2005), and the Andhra Pradesh State Government Award (2007).

**Savithri Rajeevan** teaches at the Sree Sankaracharya University of Sanskrit, Kalady, and is Vice Chairperson, Lalitha Kala Academy, Kerala. She has published two volumes of poetry, *Cherivu* (1993), and *Dehantharam* (1999). Her poetry has appeared in various anthologies, and she received the Udaya Bharati National Award for poetry in 1994.

**Ravulapalli Suneeta** writes poetry, short stories and novels. Her published works include a poetry anthology, *Anveshi* (1995), and novels *Vrutti* (1991); *Death Sentence* (1996); and *Jeevana Sandhya* (2004); and a short story anthology *Vaividhyam* (2005).

**Kutti Revathi** is the pen name of Dr S. Revathy, author of three books of poetry: *Puunaiyai Pola Alaiyum Veliccham* (2000); *Mulaigal* (2002); and *Thanimaiyin Aayiram Irakkaigal* (2003). She is also the editor of *Panikkudam*, a literary quarterly for women's writing, the first feminist magazine in Tamil. She received the Sigaram 15: Faces of the Future Award for literature from the Tamil weekly, *India Today*.

**Rose Mary** was born in 1956 in Kottayam, Kerala, and worked as a journalist and television reporter. She has published two collections of poetry, *Vakkukal Chekkerunnidam* (Where Words Roost), and *Chanju Peyyunna Mazha* (The Slanting Rain).

**Sa Usha** was born in 1954 and taught at various colleges under the University of Mysore, before she retired. She has three collections of poetry and a novel to her credit. The volumes of poetry are: *Togalu Gombeya Atma Kathe* (Autobiography of a Puppet); *Ee Neladahadu* (Song of the Earth) and *Havala Haarida Hottu* (When the Coral Flew), and the novel is *Kasuuti* (Embroidery).

**Mamta Sagar** is a poet, playwright and academic, teaching at the Centre for Kannada Studies, Bangalore University. She has published three collections of poetry, including *Kaada Navilina Hejje* (1992) and *Nadiya Neerina Teya* (1999), and four plays. Translated into various languages (including Hindi, Telugu, English and French), Sagar has been widely anthologised.

**Salma** is the author of two books of poetry: *Oru Maalaiyum Innoru Maalaiyum* (An Evening and Another Evening, 2000), and *Pachchai Devatha* (Green Angel, 2003). More recently, she has also tried her hand at short fiction and the novel.

**Mandrakanta Sen** has published six novels, a collection of short stories and ten books of poetry, including a verse-drama and rhymes for children. Three of her books of poetry are: *Hriday Abadhya Meye* (1999); *Chhadma Puran, Utsarito Alo* (2001); and *Barshaphalake Gantha Har, Kavya Sangraha* (2004). *Jhanpatal* (2000), *Sahabastan* (2003), and *Andhakar Samudrer Niche* (2004) are among her novels, and *Galper Boi* (2001) is a collection of short stories. She has been awarded the Ananda Puraskar (1999), and the Krittibas Puraskar (2003), among others.

**Mithu Sen**, artist and poet, has published two volumes of poetry: *Ma Jai Boluk* (Whatever Mother Says, 2000), and *Basmati Sharir Bagan Ba Gaan* (Basmati Body Garden or Song, 1995-2005). Her poems have appeared in magazines like *Desh* and *Jignasha*, and in English translation in *Atlas*.

**Rajee Seth** has published seven collections of short stories, and the novels *Tatsam* (1983) and *Nishkavach* (available in English translation as *Unarmed*, 1998). She has also translated two collections of Rainer Maria Rilke's letters into Hindi, and several poems by Octavio Paz and Lakshmi Kannan.

**Shahjahana** is a young poet whose significance derives from the fact that she is a Muslim writing in Telugu. Strongly critical of the oppression of women within her community, she received the Rangavalli Memorial Prize in 2000.

**Malika Amar Sheikh** is a well-known writer in Marathi. Her volumes of poetry, *Valucha Priyakar* (1979); *Mahanagar* (1999); and *Deharutu* (1999) have been critically acclaimed. She is also highly regarded for her controversial autobiography, *Mala Udhvasta Vhaychai* (1984).

**Menka Shivdasani** is a founder member of the Poetry Circle, which began in Mumbai in 1986. Her first book of poems, *Nirvana at Ten Rupees*, was published in 1990, and her second, *Stet*, appeared in 2003. She has co-translated *Freedom and Fissures*, an anthology of Sindhi poetry (1998).

**Suganthi Subramanian** wrote poetry as an expression of her understanding of her own place in the world. Married to engineer Subrabharathi Subramanian who encouraged her writing, she passed away in February 2009.

**Sukirtharani** teaches in a government school in Vellore district. She has three collections of poems to her credit: *Kaipattri En Kanavugal* (2002); *Iravumirugam* (2004), and *Avalai Mozhipeyarttaal* (2006).

**Anitha Thampi**, a chemical engineer by profession, has been publishing poetry since 1987. She has been widely translated and has represented Malayalam poetry at national and international events. Among her published works is *Muttamadikkumpol* (Sweeping the Courtyard), 2004.

**Vaidehi** is the pen name of Janaki Srinivasa Murthy. She is the author of numerous short stories, a newspaper column, and a novel, *Gulabi Talkies* (2006). A significant presence in Kannada literature, Vaidehi has published two collections of poetry: *Bindu Bindige* (1990) and *Parijatha* (1999).

**Vatsala** retired as a systems engineer from the Indian Institute of Technology, Chennai, in 1999. Starting to write at the age of forty-eight, she has published two books: *Suyam*, a collection of poems (2000), and *Vattathul*, a novel (2006). Her poems, short stories and articles have appeared in *Subha Mangala*, *Kanaizhayi* and *Pudiya Parvai.*

**Archana Varma**, poet and writer, teaches Hindi at Miranda College, Delhi University, and is Associate Editor of the Hindi literary magazine, *Hans.*

**Vijayalakshmi** works with Bharat Sanchar Nigam in Cochin. She has published eight collections of poetry, among which are *The Beast Trainer* (1992); *Some Other Face of the Rain* (1999); *A Single Grain of Sand* (2003); and, recently, *Beyond the Rain* (2009). She was awarded the Kerala Sahitya Akademi Award for poetry in 1994.

**Vimala** has been a member of the Revolutionary Writer's Association from 1979. Convenor of the Mahila Organising Committee of the CPI (ML), (1986-1990) and General Secretary of the Progressive Women's Organisation, she was the working editor of *Vimochana* and *Stree Vimukti* for several years. Her poetry anthologies include *Adavi Uppongina Raatri* (1990) and *Mrigana* (2009).

**Volga** is the pseudonym of P. Lalitha Kumari, whose novel *Sveccha* received the Chatura Novel Competition Award in 1987. Editor of the first volume of feminist philosophy in Telugu, *Maku Godalu Levu,* and an anthology of poems, *Neeli Meghalu,* she also co-edited *Sarihaddulu Leni Sandhyalu,* which addresses feminist political praxis in Andhra Pradesh. Two of her novels are *Manavi* and *Akasham lo Sagam,* and *Prayagam* is an anthology of short stories. She was awarded the first prize in the Chatura Novel Competition in 1987, and received the Nandi Award for best writer for the film *Thodu.*

# TRANSLATORS

**J. P. Das** has been a part of the Oriya literary scene for the last three decades in the genres of poetry, fiction, drama and criticism. He is the author of eleven collections of poetry, eight of which have been published in Hindi translation. Among them are *Pratham Purush* (1971), and *Alimalika* (1993). He received the Sahitya Akademi Award in 1991 for his anthology, *Ahanik.*

**Sanjukta Dasgupta** is Contributing Editor for Muse India, and has been chairperson and co-judge for the Commonwealth Writers' Prize. She is Professor of English, Calcutta University, and Dean of the Faculty of Arts.

**J. Devika** is Associate Professor and member of the Board of Studies, Women's Studies, University of Calicut. She also acts as editorial advisor to the first women's publishing house in Malayalam, Women's Imprint, and is also an advisor on the Stories Project, Anveshi, Hyderabad. She has translated Nalini Jameela's *Oru Laingikatozhilaaliyude Athmakatha* (Autobiography of a Sex Worker, 2005).

**Mehr Afshan Farooqi** is Assistant Professor at the Department of Middle Eastern and South Asian Languages and Cultures, University of Virginia. She is the editor of the two-volume Oxford *Anthology of Modern Urdu Literature* (2008), covering prose, fiction and poetry.

**V. Geetha** writes in Tamil and English on Tamil history, culture and society, and on gender. Among her books are *Gender* (2000); *Soul Force: Gandhi's Writings on Peace* (2004); *Patriarchy* (2007); and with S.V. Rajadurai, *Towards a Non-Brahmin Millennium: From Iyothee Thass to Periyar* (2008). She is the editorial director of Tara Publishing.

**Madhu B. Joshi** has translated several books from English into Hindi, including M.N. Srinivas's *Indian Village,* Mrinal Pande's *Devi,* and Germaine Greer's *The Female Eunuch,* as well as several major Hindi poets and writers to English.

**Udaya Kumar** is Professor of English, Delhi University. His publications include *The Joycean Labyrinth: Repetition, Time and*

*Tradition in Ulysses*, and several papers on Indian literature, life-writing, and literary theory. He is currently working on a new book, *Styles of the Self: The Subject and the Act of Self-Articulation in Modern Malayalam Writing*.

**Sachin Ketkar** writes poetry in both Marathi and English. He has translated and edited *Live Update: An Anthology of Recent Marathi Poetry* (2005), and is Reader in the Department of English of Maharaja Sayajirao University, Baroda.

**Subashree Krishnaswamy** edited the *Indian Review of Books*, a monthly magazine devoted to book reviews, for a number of years. She translates fiction and poetry written in Tamil, into English and now teaches at the Asian College of Journalism, Chennai. She has co-edited, with K. Srilata, *Seablue Child: Short Fiction from South India* (2007), and an anthology of Tamil poetry in translation entitled *The Rapids of a Great River: The Penguin Book of Tamil Poetry* (2009).

**Shirin Kuchedkar** was the Head, Department of English, SNDT Women's University, Mumbai, for 14 years. She has written extensively on feminist literary criticism and women writers. Among other published work, she edited *Postmodernism and Feminism: Canadian Context*, and co-edited *Violence Against Women*. She passed away in March 2009.

**A. Mangai** is the pseudonym of V. Padma, who has been actively engaged in Tamil theatre as an actor, director and playwright for over two decades. Writing in Tamil and English, her publications include entries in *The Oxford Companion to Indian Theatre* (2004), a translation of her play, *Pani-t-Thee as 'Frozen Fire' in Staging Resistance: Plays by Women* (2004), and *Penniya Arasiyal*, a monograph on feminist politics (2005).

**Sitanshu Yashaschandra Mehta** is among contemporary Gujarati literature's most eminent representatives. Poet, playwright, translator and academic, he has received several awards over the years, including the Sahitya Akademi Award (1987) for his significant opus, *Jatayu*, and the Padma Shri (2006). He is the author of three books of poetry.

**Ritu Menon** is co-founder of Kali for Women, India's oldest feminist press, and of Women Unlimited, an associate of Kali for Women. She has written and published widely on women, and is co-author of *Borders & Boundaries: Women in India's Partition (1998); and Unequal*

*Citizens: A Study of Muslim Women in India (2004)* with Zoya Hasan. She has also edited several anthologies of women's writing in India.

**Hoshang Merchant** has lived and taught in Heidelberg, Iran and Jerusalem, studied Buddhism at the Tibetan Library at Dharamsala, and Islam in Iran and Palestine. He teaches Poetry and Surrealism at the University of Hyderabad, and has published 13 works of poetry, among them: *Flower to Flame* (1989); *The Home, the Friend and the World* (1995); *Bellagio Blues* (2004); and *Homage to Jibanananda Das* (2005). He is also the author of two books of critical studies, and the editor of the volume *Yaarana: Gay Writing from India* (1999).

**K. Ayyappa Paniker**, poet, professor and critic, is among the pioneers of modernism in Kerala, whose critical writing covers poetry and literary criticism, film and film-making, theatre and other visual arts. Among his works of poetry are *Days and Nights*, and *I Can't Help Blossoming*. His translations include *Medieval Indian Literature* in English Translation, and the *Complete Works of Shakespeare* in Malayalam. He passed away in 2006.

**Chitra Panikkar** was previously faculty at the Centre for Translation Studies, University of Hyderabad, and now teaches in the English Department of Bangalore University.

**Suguna Ramanathan** is Professor, Department of English, St. Xaviers College, Ahmedabad. She has published two books of critical studies, *Iris Murdoch: Figures of Good* and *The Novels of C.P. Snow: a Critical Introduction*, as well as a book of Gujarati poetry in translation. She is also co-author and co-editor of a study of Dalit women in the Bhal region of Gujarat.

**A. K. Ramanujan** was a scholar of Indian literature who wrote in both English and Kannada. With a large body of astonishingly varied work, Ramanujan wore many hats; philologist, folklorist, translator, poet and playwright. His academic research ranged across five languages: Tamil, Kannada, Telugu, Sanskrit and English, including works on both classical and modern variants of these literatures. Among his best known translations are *Speaking of Siva* (1973) and *Hymns for the Drowning* (1981).

**Sudeep Sen**'s recent work appears in *New Writing 15* (2007); *Language for a New Century* (2008); and *Leela: An Erotic Play of Verse* *and Art* (2009). He is the editor of the literary magazine, *Atlas*, and editorial director of AARK ARTS. He has translated *Spellbound & Other Poems – Fazal Shahabuddin* (2003), and *Love & Other Poems by Aminur Rahman* (2001), among other works.

**Aruna Sitesh** is Principal of Indraprastha College for Women, University of Delhi. She co-edits the quarterly *Pratibha India*, and has published five collections of Hindi short stories. Recent publications include *Glimpses: The Modern Indian Short Story* and *Beyond Gender and Geography: American Women Writers - Modern Short Stories.*

**K. Srilata** teaches at the Indian Institute of Technology, Chennai. Her books include *The Other Half of the Coconut: Women Writing Self-Respect History*, and an anthology of poetry, *Seablue Child: Short Fiction from South India,* co-edited with Subashree Krishnaswamy (2007). She has also co-edited, with Subashree Krishnaswamy, an anthology of Tamil poetry in translation titled *The Rapids of a Great River: The Penguin Book of Tamil Poetry* (2009).

**Ramachandra Sharma**, poet, dramatist, writer of short stories and translator, is a pioneer of the modernist movement in Kannada poetry and has played a significant role in the making of Navya fiction. He has also translated a hundred English poems of this century, a novel by Masti, and a collection of 13 short stories by Yashwant Chittal into Kannada.

**C. S. Venkiteswaran** is director of the School of Media Studies, Kochi. Apart from his substantial contribution to translation, he is also a well-known film critic, and now a member of the Kerala State Film Akademi.

**Arlene Zide** teaches at the City Colleges of Chicago, and is an acclaimed translator. Her translations from Hindi and other Indian languages have appeared in *Indian Literature, The Malahat Review, International Quarterly*, and *Translation Review*. Her book, *In Their Own Voice: An Anthology of Contemporary Indian Women Poets*, was published in 1993. She has a forthcoming work entitled *Anthology of Hindi Women Poets* (2009).